THERESE & JACQUIE FINLAY

Authors Thérèse and Jacquie Finlay
Editors Jane Bishop and Susan Howard
Assistant editor Lesley Sudlow
Series designer Lynne Joesbury
Designer Rachael Hammond
Illustrations Claire Boyce
Cover Lynne Joesbury
Action Rhymes, Poems and Stories compiled by Jackie Andrews
Songs compiled by Peter Morrell
Assemblies chapter by Lesley Prior

Designed using Adobe Pagemaker
Processed by Scholastic Ltd, Leamington Spa

Published by Scholastic Ltd, Villiers House, Clarendon Avenue, Leamington Spa, Warwickshire CV32 5PR

1 2 3 4 5 6 7 8 9 9 0 1 2 3 4 5 6 7 8

The publishers gratefully acknowledge permission to reproduce the following copyright material:
Jackie Andrews for 'The newspaper princess' © 1999, Jackie Andrews, previously unpublished; **Ann Bryant** for 'The big bad wolf' © 1999, Ann Bryant, previously unpublished; **Susan Eames** for 'Paper' and 'Tap, tap, tap' © 1999, Susan Eames, previously unpublished; **John Foster** for 'What are they like?' © 1999, John Foster, previously unpublished and 'There's a hole in my pants' from *Clothes Poems* © 1991, John Foster (1991, OUP); **Jean Gilbert** for '1, 2, 3, 4, Ev'rybody play' © 1999, Jean Gilbert, previously unpublished; **Trevor Harvey** for 'Materials' © 1999, Trevor Harvey, previously unpublished; **Hazel Hobbs** for 'Favourite fabrics' and 'Plastic' © 1999, Hazel Hobbs, previously unpublished; **Johanne Levy** for 'Building' © 1999 Johanne Levy, previously unpublished; **Tony Mitton** for 'Playdough people' © 1999, Tony Mitton, previously unpublished; **David Moses** for 'Paper comes from trees' © 1999, David Moses, previously unpublished; **Sue Nicholls** for 'Hexagons' (Patchwork calypso) © 1999, Sue Nicholls, previously unpublished; **Peggy Vance of The Writer's Bureau** as Literary Representative for Claire Nielson for 'Polly and the patchwork quilt' © 1999, Claire Nielson, previously unpublished; **Jan Pollard** for 'The kitchen band', 'Move like a robot' and 'The wooden house' © 1999, Jan Pollard, previously unpublished; **Lesley Prior** for assemblies © 1999, Lesley Prior, previously unpublished; **Coral Rumble** for 'Blowing glass' © 1999, Coral Rumble, previously unpublished; **Pat Sweet** for 'Rub a dub dub' © 1999, Pat Sweet, previously unpublished; **Stevie Ann Wilde** for 'Swinging' and 'Brand new' © 1999, Stevie Ann Wilde, previously unpublished; **Brenda Williams** for 'Patterns', 'Build a house with bricks' and 'Trees' © 1999, Brenda Williams, previously unpublished; **Irene Yates** for 'Little wooden truck' © 1999, Irene Yates, previously unpublished.
Every effort has been made to trace copyright holders and the publishers apologize for any inadvertent omissions.

British Library Cataloguing-in-Publication Data A catalogue record for this book is available from the British Library.

ISBN 0-590-53864-0

CONTENTS

CHAPTER 6: BUILDING MATERIALS

CHAPTER 7: DISPLAYS

CHAPTER 8: ASSEMBLIES

RESOURCES

POEMS AND ACTION RHYMES

STORIES

SONGS

ACTIVITY SHEETS

INTRODUCTION

The world around us is made up of a vast assortment of materials which can provide a fascinating topic for young children to explore! As the educators of young children we need to stimulate and foster an appreciation of the world around them and of what that world consists. Many children do not comprehend the meaning of the word 'materials', thinking it only relates to fabrics, they need to appreciate that the word encompasses substances they use and see every day such as paper, wood, plastics, metals and building materials.

Encourage your children to be curious of their natural environment, by using a familiar context, object or material to teach them about their world.

As we all become more environmentally aware, the activities in this book will encourage the children to foster positive attitudes to protecting our planet.

As a theme 'Materials' aims to make young children aware of properties and range in an exciting and fun way, where the child is at the centre of all discoveries. Throughout the book the children will encounter a broad range of concepts, skills and attitudes in all areas of the curriculum.

LOOKING AT MATERIALS

The varied range of activities provided in this book ensure that the children investigate the properties of given materials rather than the properties of the object they are looking at, including the strength, absorbency and magnetism.

Chapter 1 (Paper) encourages the children to discover the origin and uses of paper. In Chapter 2 (Metals), they consider the different types of metals along with some of their products, with the children being given the opportunity to determine how these metals are used for a wide range of purposes. In Chapter 3 (Fabrics), children look at some of the properties of fabrics with activities to investigate absorbency and the need for waterproofing. They are encouraged to raise questions, thus promoting their language development. Chapter 4 (Wood) provides opportunities for the children to design their own picture frames, examine the parts of a tree and study the different animals who depend on trees. In Chapter 5 (Plastics), environmental issues are raised and discussed with the children. Through structured play, floating and sinking and capacity are explored. In Chapter 6 (Building Materials), activities consider safety issues along with the roles of trades people and the materials they require.

Although the theme 'Materials' naturally lends itself to scientific-based activities, all ten areas of the curriculum are covered in an integrated approach, with cross-curricular links especially through discussion and follow-up work (see Topic web on pages 8 and 9 which shows the curriculum areas covered by each activity).

HOW TO USE THIS BOOK

Themes for Early Years – 'Materials' is one of a series of books written for early years educators of children aged between three and six years old. It can be used when working with young children at home, in playgroups, nurseries, nursery classes and schools.

Young children learn best when they are given opportunities to use all their senses and engage in activities which appeal to their natural curiosity. It is important that children feel secure and able to express themselves in a safe and relaxed environment while they are learning.

This book is a comprehensive resource pack providing all you will need to tackle a topic on this theme; from activity ideas to suggestions for displays and assemblies. However, the book is organized to allow flexibility and means that you can use the resources either for a long-term project or a few activities at a time to support work on a particular material.

However you choose to use the resources, they can be adapted to suit the needs of the young children in your care.

TOPIC WEB

The Topic web on pages 8 and 9 is photocopiable and organized to assist planning, ensuring a broad and balanced curriculum. Each activity, while having cross-curricular links, also relates to the National Curriculum and Scottish 5–14 Guidelines.

ACTIVITY PAGES

Each of the first six chapters outlines activities to develop awareness and understanding of different types of materials: paper, metal, fabric, wood, plastic and building materials. Each activity follows a set format and is linked to a specific curriculum area, for which a learning objective is highlighted. This objective explains the purpose of the activity, and where possible uses language from the National Curriculum. Guidelines are given for appropriate group sizes for each activity, however this is flexible depending upon the level of adult support you can provide and other circumstances. A list of necessary resources are supplied along with notes outlining any preparation you will need to carry out before starting the activity.

In 'What to do', step-by-step instructions describe each activity in detail. Generally the activities can be adapted to suit different ability levels. Relevant points for discussion are highlighted and this should help encourage all the children to actively engage in developing their ideas and expanding their vocabulary.

Follow-up ideas for extending each activity are also listed, these may support the specific curriculum area or introduce new areas of learning.

DISPLAYS

Displays should be central to the children's work providing a focal point for the children to contribute to a particular theme. Where possible, displays should encourage literacy through speaking and listening, posing relevant questions and encouraging reading and writing activities.

As a purpose of display is to enhance and create an interesting environment, they should be inviting and at the children's level if at all possible. This section highlights some specific displays on the 'Materials' theme.

ASSEMBLIES

Irrespective of denominations within your group of children, this chapter provides ideas for assemblies or group sharing time based on the theme of 'Materials'. Each assembly has its own practical ideas on how the children can be encouraged to contribute and reflect on the specific theme. Relevant prayers and songs are suggested.

RESOURCES

A useful selection of stories, poems, action rhymes and songs linked to 'Materials' are provided in this section. Much of the material is new and has been especially commissioned to complement the topic. All of these resources are photocopiable.

PHOTOCOPIABLE SHEETS

Eight photocopiable pages which are each related to a previous activity in the book are provided. Make sure that the instructions are clearly understood and that any new vocabulary is fully explained before handing out the sheets. Build in opportunities to discuss the completed work and the depth of understanding.

RECOMMENDED MATERIALS

The final page in the book provides a list of useful, additional resource material in the form of story books, information books, song and poetry books.

EXPRESSIVE ARTS

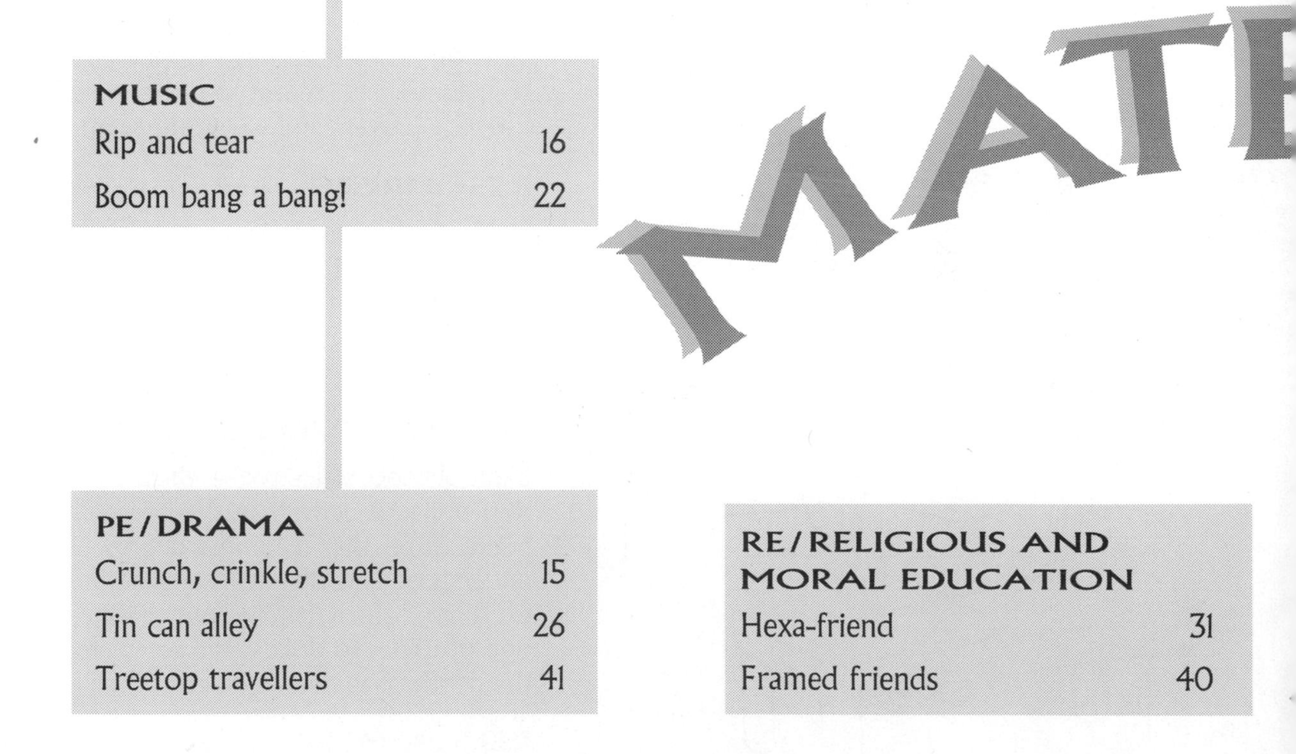

Planning towards the National Curriculum and the Scottish National guidelines 5–14

MATHEMATICS

HISTORY / PEOPLE IN THE PAST

ENVIRONMENTAL STUDIES

SCIENCE

DESIGN AND TECHNOLOGY

GEOGRAPHY / PEOPLE AND PLACES

PREPARING FOR PRIMARY SCHOOL

The National Curriculum was established to standardize the subjects and subject content taught at all levels of a child's education. It is intended that any child will be able to go to a school throughout the country and find the same areas of the curriculum being covered for the same amount of time every week. The National Curriculum subjects are: English, Mathematics, Science and ICT (the core subjects), Art, Design and Technology, Geography, History, Music and PE (the foundation subjects) and RE.

Each activity has a specific learning objective which is linked to the relevant National Curriculum subject area. It is important not to overlook the value of learning through the medium of play; the activities described here place an emphasis on sensory learning, discussion and physical activity.

TOWARDS LEVEL ONE

Although children under the age of five do not have to fulfil the requirements of the National Curriculum, they are working towards Level 1 while following their own curriculum outlined through the Desirable Outcomes for children's learning, prescribed by the Qualifications and Curriculum Authority.

The guidelines divide the curriculum into six main areas – Personal and Social Development, Language and Literacy, Mathematics, Knowledge and Understanding of the World, Physical Development and Creative Development.

All these areas of learning can be approached through a range of structured, imaginative and free play activities which all prepare for the subjects of the National Curriculum.

Most nurseries will find that the experiences they are offering will provide a good foundation for the curriculum their children will follow once they are in school. The activities outlined in the book will help you prepare children for many aspects of it, and they will also fit well into the pre-five curriculum guidelines issued by local authorities throughout Scotland.

THE SCOTTISH GUIDELINES 5–14

In Scotland, there are National Guidelines for schools on what should be taught to children between the ages of five and fourteen.

These National Guidelines are divided into six main curriculum areas: English Language, Mathematics, Environmental Studies, Expressive Arts, Religious and Moral Education, Personal and Social Development.

Within these main areas, further subjects are found, for example, 'Expressive Arts' includes art and design, drama, music and PE. Strands are also identified within each subject, for example Mathematics includes problem-solving, enquiry, and shape, position and movement.

PLANNING

To help with planning, the activities described here have been organized into separate areas of the curriculum on the Topic web on pages 8 and 9. The children's personal and social development is an ongoing theme that is incorporated throughout the activities in this book.

CHAPTER 1
PAPER

Children make use of paper every day for drawing, writing, in books and comics. In this chapter, they will find out all about it and will have the opportunity to make wallpaper books, bags and old maps and discover how paper is made and used.

PAPER PATTERNS

Objective

Mathematics – To recognize and create a recurring pattern.

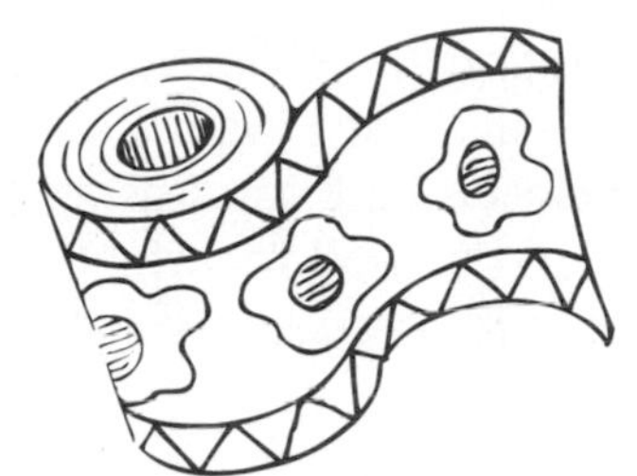

Group size

Small groups.

What you need

Selection of wallpaper borders showing a repetitive pattern, strips of white paper (approximately 60cm × 15cm), mixed paint in various colours, shapes to print with, selection of templates, drawing and colouring materials, selection of objects to create a practical pattern (beads, blocks, animal shapes, vehicles), items of clothing (hats, scarves, gloves and coats).

Preparation

Cut and display strips of border, ensuring the repeating pattern is obvious for the children to see. Ensure the work surface is protected and resources made available for the children to use.

What to do

Introduce the concept of repeating patterns by using the children to create practical patterns such as boy, girl, boy, girl, or standing, kneeling, standing, kneeling and so on. Encourage them to make their own practical patterns using the items of clothing. Provide opportunities to copy and complete a pattern which has been started.

Now let the children look closely at the selection of wallpaper borders and encourage them to pay particular attention to the pattern and how it repeats. Explain that a person who creates the patterns for the borders is called a designer and when they make a new wallpaper border they have to devise a pattern making sure it is repeated. Suggest that they are to become wallpaper designers and before they go into production they have to create a practical pattern which repeats. Supply the children with a selection of objects to experiment with to make repeating patterns such as bead, block, bead, block, or cow, sheep, cow, sheep.

Once the children have grasped the concept of a repeating pattern, challenge them to design their own wallpaper borders using drawings, templates or shapes to print onto strips of paper. These patterns can be simple or complex depending upon the children's skills.

Discussion

Ask the children to describe a repeating pattern. How does it repeat? How many colours do you need to use? How many shapes do you need to use? Can you see any repeating patterns where you live? Which room could you use this border in? Think about the pattern used. Would you put a border with dummies and rattles on it in your living room? What would you like on your bedroom border?

Follow-up activities

✧ Display finished borders in a role-play setting.
✧ Make the completed borders into wallpaper books to be used in a 'Wallpaper shop'.
✧ Encourage the children to work in pairs, creating more complex wallpaper designs.

WHICH GOES WHERE?

Objective

Science – To recognize properties of different types of paper and begin to notice similarities and differences.

Group size

Small groups.

What you need

Selection of different coloured and different textured papers (crêpe, tissue, tracing, sugar, cartridge, card, wrapping paper, kitchen paper, wallpaper, brown paper, corrugated cardboard). Large pieces of plain paper, glue and writing materials to record results.

Preparation

Cut paper into manageable pieces.

What to do

Introduce one type of paper to the children, encouraging them to use all their senses to explore it. Enhance their exploration by asking them questions such as: Is it noisy? Is it smooth or bumpy? Can you see through it? Can you blow it along the floor?

Follow the same procedure using a different piece of paper, challenging the children to highlight any similarities or differences when compared with the first type. Consider all the remaining papers, sorting them into sets using a range of properties such as transparent, translucent, rough, smooth, colour, thickness and so on.

Attach a sample piece of each paper onto a large sheet of paper and record any appropriate words that the children may suggest to describe the paper or its properties.

Provide the children with a property such as thickness, and challenge them to place the paper in the correct order from the thickest to the thinnest.

Discussion

Question the children as to which paper would make the best windows for a doll's house? Which would be best for making books? Which paper would be good for wrapping up presents? Stress the need to qualify their answers with supportive reasons why.

Follow-up activities

✧ Design a 'paper' book for each type of paper, incorporating a wide spectrum of language to describe its properties and uses.
✧ Use the different papers for displays as collaged scenes or textured pictures.
✧ Use translucent paper to create a stained glass window effect, overlapping different colours to make new shades.
✧ Teach and display the poem 'Paper' by Susan Eames on page 69.

HOW IS IT MADE?

Objectives

Geography – To recognize that some materials exist naturally and some are manufactured; to realize that some materials need to be processed.

Group size

Small groups.

What you need

A story book, an exercise book, a pencil, a wooden ruler, twigs and leaves, photocopiable page 89, card and writing materials.

Preparation

Group and display the above resources (which all link to trees). Prepare card into folded labels and photocopy page 89 to provide one copy per child.

What to do

Discuss with the children each of the objects in your collection, encouraging them to write labels using emergent writing. Ask the children what links all these things together, paying close attention to what they are made from. If the children fail to recognize the common factor, explain they all come from trees, even the paper! Provide the

children with an outline of the paper-making process using the following guidelines:

- trees are grown
- trees are chopped down
- they are taken over the land or water to processing factories
- at the factory they are chopped and worked to a pulp
- the pulp is flattened and left to dry as paper.

Provide each child with a photocopiable sheet and explain they have to cut, colour and stick the pictures in the correct order to represent the paper-making process. Ensure the children know where to start when displaying their correct order – working from left to right.

Discussion

Ask the children about the areas where trees are grown, what are they called? How are the trees cut down? Do the people plant new trees when they cut them down? How old are the trees when they are cut down? Are the trees important for anything else? Who lives in trees? What types of trees can you name? What do they shout when they chop the trees down? Why? Is all paper the same quality?

Follow-up activities

✧ Discuss what recycled paper is? What are the benefits? Why isn't all paper recycled?
✧ Investigate other natural materials and how they are processed (wool, rubber, coal).
✧ Challenge the children to discover what originates from the sea, the land and underground.
✧ Teach the children the song 'Paper comes from trees' in the Resource section on page 84.

LET'S GO SHOPPING

Objectives

Science – To determine the most appropriate material for a shopping bag; to understand the importance of fair testing.

Group size

Small groups working in pairs.

What you need

Scissors, stapler, glue, Sellotape, selection of paper bags, fruit to carry and a selection of different papers (tissue, crêpe, cartridge, sugar, tracing) all in A4.

Preparation

Look at the selection of paper bags with the children and discuss their properties. How are the bags sealed? How many openings are there? Are they all the same size?

What to do

Tell the children the grocer has no paper bags left in his shop: how can we help? Encourage them to look at the available materials and think about how to make the bags. Challenge each pair of children to choose a different type of paper to make a bag.

Let the children make their bags using the different papers and then compare their bags with each other. Which bag do you think is the strongest? Which is the best bag and why? Emphasize the need for proof of which is the strongest, to make it a fair test. Suggest placing the same items of fruit in each bag and carrying them the same distance to test.

Discussion

How could you illustrate the sides of your bags to indicate what the bag contains? Might you need larger bags? Why? What other types of bags could you test?

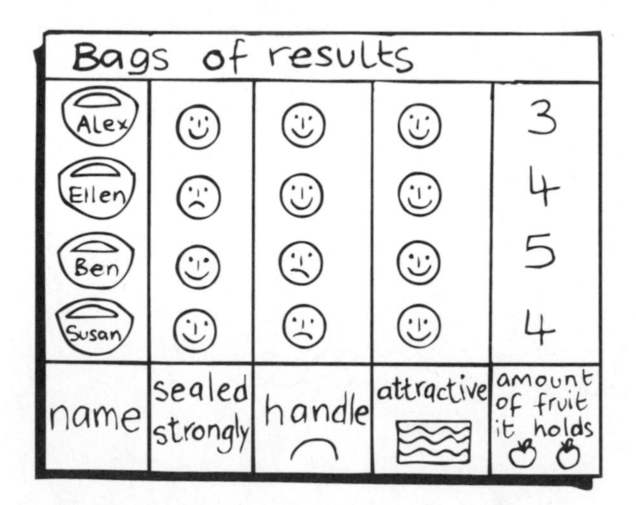

Bags of results

name	sealed strongly	handle	attractive	amount of fruit it holds
Alex	☺	☺	☺	3
Ellen	☹	☺	☺	4
Ben	☺	☹	☺	5
Susan	☺	☹	☺	4

Follow-up activities

✧ Make carrier bags complete with a handle, using a wider range of fastenings.
✧ Test the strength of paper in other ways by making structures.
✧ Devise a chart to record the properties of different bags, using happy and sad faces (above).

CRUNCH, CRINKLE, STRETCH

Objective

PE – To explore types of movement and develop them into a sequence.

Group size

Any size.

What you need

A large space, tambourine or other percussion instrument, large sheets of paper (different varieties).

Preparation

Gather the children into a circle, demonstrating what you can make the paper do; such as squash into a ball, stretch into a flat shape, crinkle to make a noise, tear to make jagged edges, rip quickly and so on.

What to do

To warm up, invite the children to travel about the space in different ways and directions, guided by you. Encourage them to use all the space available both when travelling and stopping.

When the children are warmed up, explain that they are going to curl up small and when the tambourine is shaken, stretch out slowly into flat shapes to represent the movement of the paper they previously observed.

Stress that a stretch can either be lying on their front or back, arms and legs together or outstretched, standing up to make a tall thin shape or a short wide shape, or stretching with one hand and one foot on the floor.

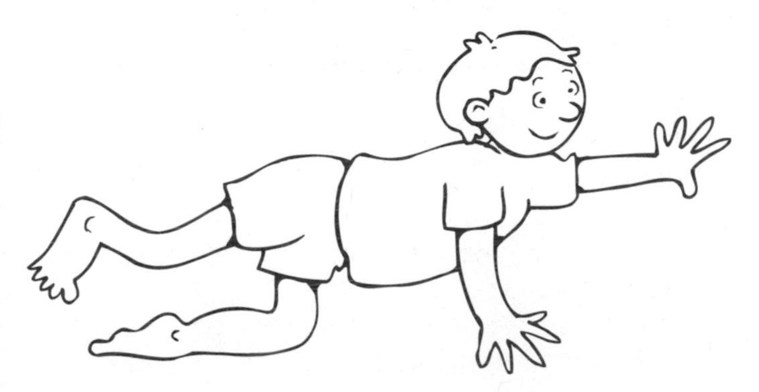

Practise this several times and then encourage them to curl up small. Ensure they realize that they have to be as 'crunched' as the paper by tucking arms and legs as close to their body as possible. Challenge them to have a different part of their body touching the floor each time (back, side, knees, toes).

After opportunities to practise these movements independently, explain to them they are now to move around the room curled up and when the tambourine is shaken they have to stretch out, to stimulate the 'crunch, crinkle, stretch' of the paper.

Once the children have gained confidence in this movement, provide opportunities for them to develop their own sequence using curls and stretches. Where appropriate use demonstration to highlight good practice.

Discussion

Talk to the children about the papers and ask them questions such as: Do they make a noise? Do all the papers make the same noise? Which sound do you like the best? Which paper can you crunch or crinkle up the smallest? Does the paper look the same after it has been scrunched? Can you scrunch with one hand or two?

Follow-up activities

✧ Develop this activity to include hoops for the children to curl and stretch in. Make the commands more difficult or decrease the number of hoops each time the game is played.

✧ Consider other materials, how their shape can be altered and challenge the children to make their movements reflect this.

✧ Encourage the children to write, demonstrate or draw their sequence for a friend to follow.

RIP AND TEAR

Objective

Music – To recognize the differences between long and short sounds.

Group size

Any size; working in pairs.

What you need

Large amounts of scrap paper (including foil, tracing, tissue, crêpe).

Preparation

Cut paper into long and short pieces. Gather the children together.

What to do

Show the paper to the children asking them how they are different. Once it has been established that they are various lengths, encourage the children to investigate making noises with them. Following this demonstrate how the paper may be ripped or torn. Challenge them to determine which is a long or short sound, emphasizing the relationship between the length of the paper and the sound.

Provide opportunities for the children to work in pairs. One child hides and tears the paper (out of view), while their partner guesses whether they used a long or short piece of paper.

Following this, encourage the children to work in pairs and discover other paper sounds, including blowing across different papers, scrunching, shaking, wafting and crinkling. Develop this by making various shakers using foil, tracing, crêpe and tissue papers either scrunched or rolled to make different sounds.

Discussion

Ask the children whether the thickness/quality of the paper makes a difference to the sound which is produced? Which paper is the easiest to tear? What other sounds can you make with the paper? Can you make a quiet sound? What makes the loudest sound?

Follow-up activities

✧ Introduce percussion instruments to make long and short sounds.

✧ Use a stopwatch to determine which sound is the longest and shortest. Represent these results on different graphs.

✧ Investigate which child can make the longest sound with their voice.

HUNT FOR TREASURE

Objectives

Geography – To recognize common features of maps and to use this information to make a map; to consider the most suitable paper for maps.

Group size

Small groups.

What you need

Selection of different maps (road maps, Ordnance Survey maps, aerial maps, treasure maps), paper in different colours, types and sizes, drawing and colouring materials.

Preparation

Make up and tell the children a story about Peter Pirate who was sailing the high seas seeking treasure, when suddenly, a huge wave tossed poor Peter Pirate into the cold, dark, deep sea. Peter Pirate eventually found his way to an island where he believed there to be treasure.

What to do

Discuss with the children Peter Pirate's predicament. He realizes that there is treasure but he is unable to find it. What could he use to help him?

Hopefully the children should suggest the use of a map. Challenge them to make a map of the island to help Peter Pirate find the treasure, allowing them to make their own decisions as to size, colour, form, landmarks and so on. Before

they start their own map, talk about the finished maps, deciding upon which is the clearest map and why. Introduce the published maps to the children, highlighting their specific features, such as roads, motorways, footpaths, churches, woods, lakes, rivers and so on.

Now ask the children to produce their own treasure map for Peter Pirate to follow, remembering to feature specific areas and mark the site of the treasure clearly with an X.

Discussion

Discuss with the children which paper and materials would be most suitable to use for a map. Should you be able to see through the paper? Does the ink soak through the paper? Does the paper fold easily? What would happen if the drawn map was the same colour as the paper? If the paper fell in the water what would happen?

Follow-up activities

- Dye paper before making maps using cold tea or coffee to make the map look old.
- Make maps to direct friends from home to the local shops.
- Ask the children if they could direct their friend blindfolded around the room. What kind of words would you use? Talk about when and who uses road maps. Is an Ordnance Survey map different to a road map? If so, how?
- Take photographs of the local environment for the children to place on a large scale map of the local area. Attach cardboard figures to the map and encourage the children to move these to different locations.

STRIPES AND PATTERNS

Objective

English – To use a range of adjectives to describe various wallpapers.

Group size

Small groups; working in pairs.

What you need

Photocopiable page 90, selection of different wallpapers, magnifying glasses, large paper to record ideas, felt-tipped pens, drawing and colouring materials.

Preparation

Photocopy and fold sheets to make individual booklets for each child. Display wallpapers for children to investigate.

What to do

Explain to the children that magnifying glasses are used to examine objects closely, by holding them near to the object and gently moving them away, until the item can be seen clearly.

Divide the children into pairs, providing one child in the pair with a strip of wallpaper and the other with plain paper and colouring materials. Challenge one child to use the magnifying glass to help describe in detail the piece of wallpaper. The other child, who is out of view, has to recreate the pattern on their piece of paper. Following this the children should compare their results with the rest of the group.

Throughout this process, make sure the children are clear that the best results came from using a broad range of descriptive language focusing on: colour, shape, size, pattern and pictures.

To reinforce this concept, as a group, choose a wallpaper and ask the children to supply a descriptive word in turn. Record what they say as a sentence on the large sheet of paper. For example, 'It has got a pale green background, with thin dark green stripes and placed in between the stripes are little gold stars'.

Now introduce the children to the pre-made booklets. Explain that you would like them to colour the patterns in and describe in detail each of the wallpaper patterns shown. They then should design and describe a pattern of their own on the final page of the booklet.

Discussion

Challenge the children to think of as many actual names for shades of colour, such as pink, red, ruby, cherry, scarlet, rose and so on. Are the patterns/pictures big or little, fat or thin? Is it a dark or bright paper? Does it make you feel happy or sad? Does it remind you of anywhere you have been? Would you like it in your house?

Follow-up activities

✧ Devise a game, with one child describing a given wallpaper or object to the rest of the group (who can't see it) and then asking the others to draw or describe it.

✧ Challenge the children to create a book using adjectives to describe carpet patterns.

✧ Make lists of describing words for different objects. Mount these and let the children use them as a resource.

✧ Encourage the children to think of suitable names for the different wallpaper designs.

CHAPTER 2
METALS

Through art, music, technology and physical education children can make and design pictures and people, experiment with different noises and develop their co-ordination using metal as a stimulus.

WHICH STICKS?

Objective
Science – To recognize properties of different metals; to group metals into magnetic and non-magnetic.

Group size
Small groups.

What you need
Selection of objects including magnetic and non-magnetic metals, magnets, magnifying glasses, coloured card, writing and drawing materials.

Preparation
Give the children a chance to look at all the items you have gathered together. Cut a magnet and a circle shape from card. Label the magnet shape 'Magnetic' and the circle shape 'Non-magnetic'.

Sub-divide metallic materials into magnetic and non-magnetic, and use only the magnetic metals for the initial introductory activity.

What to do
Challenge the children to predict which of the materials the magnets will attract (stick to), placing them on the magnet-shaped card and the others on the circle. Allow the children to test their predictions and make any relevant changes to where the items are placed. Refer the children to the objects on the magnet shape card and discuss why they are the same. Encourage them to contribute words such as: hard, cold, smooth, metal, magnetic and so on.

Pose the following question: 'Are all metals magnetic?'. Once a decision has been made, provide the children with magnetic and non-magnetic materials to test their hypothesis and ask them to sort them accordingly.

Discussion
Ask the children to name different metals. Can you bend metal? Is metal thick or thin? Where does metal come from? Can you find metal around the room? What happens to metal when it gets wet?

Follow-up activities
✧ Discuss different uses and purposes of metal, posing questions such as: Could scissors be made from paper not metal? Could irons be made from wood not metal?

✧ Make an interactive table-top display for the children to investigate and provide task cards such as: How many paper clips can your magnet hold? Can your magnet pick up a heavy object?

✧ Draw faces on corks, stick drawing pins in the base, stand them on card and make them dance using a magnet underneath.

WHAT DID KNIGHTS WEAR?

Objectives

History – To recognize changes over time and hear stories from the past; to develop historical language.

Group size

Any size groups.

What you need

Pictures or posters depicting knights in protective armour (if available), large sheets of paper, scissors, drawing materials and treasury tags.

Preparation

Cut a piece of paper into the shape of a breast plate to fit a child:

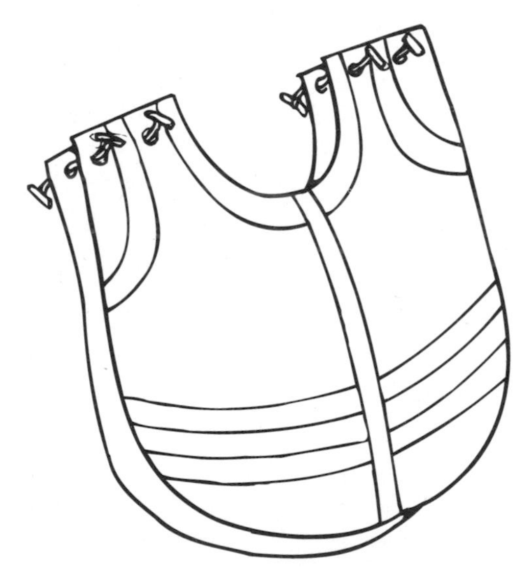

What to do

To ensure the children are familiar with historical language provide them with the following information, elaborating where necessary:

- A long time ago, there was a man known as King Arthur. He had knights who helped him.
- Sometimes they went into battle and used lances which were long, pointed poles, heavy swords and a long chain with a heavy spiky ball attached to it. Their opponents used similar weapons.
- To protect themselves the knights wore special protective armour and carried shields.

Following this, and if available, show the children pictures of knights in protective armour. Demonstrate on a child how the cut-out breastplate is worn. Do they know what it is made of? Why did the knights wear it? Would this breastplate stop the knights from being hurt?

Investigate with the children why the breastplate would need to be as hard, durable, strong and as light as possible. Ask the children why it needs to be like this and what would be the best material to make an effective breastplate from?

Explain that, as all parts of their bodies were in danger of being injured, the knights used to wear protective armour all over their body.

Use the paper and treasury tags to make 'a suit of armour' for a child. Place the treasury tags at the jointed areas to allow for movement. Ask the child to walk around the room explaining how it feels and how effective it would be in battle.

Discussion

Would you be able to run in the armour? Would it be heavy? If you fell or were knocked over could you pick yourself up? How strong is metal? Would the shields be smooth or dented and why? Do we have knights nowadays? Who would use a shield nowadays to protect themselves? What weapons are used now?

Follow-up activities

✧ Read some stories about King Arthur and the Knights of the Round Table.

✧ Talk to the children about any animals that have a 'protective armour' such as turtles and tortoises.

CLINK, CLANK

Objective

English – To write for a specific purpose.

Group size

Small groups.

What you need

Paper, envelopes, writing materials, reclaimed materials, glue, Blu-Tack, metallic silver spray, pictures of robots (if available).

Preparation

Discuss with the children the pictures of robots asking them what they think they are made from? Why do they think this? Why are robots made from metal? What colour are they? Make a 'robot' out of reclaimed materials, and spray it with metallic paint (following safety procedures on the can). Compose a letter from 'Roger Robot' (or something similar) stating where he lives and what he likes to do. Address this to the children and attach it to his hand with Blu-Tack.

What to do

Introduce the robot to the children, drawing their attention to the letter. Ask the children to predict what the robot might be called, why he has written and what the letter might contain. Open the letter and read it to the children. Suggest they may like to reply to his letter and discuss what they want to tell and ask him such as:

- Where they like to go and where does he like to go?
- How old they are and how old is he?
- Who lives in their house and where does he live?
- What they like to play and does he like to play?
- What they like to eat and what does he eat?
- The name of their best friend and has he any friends?

Use the robot's letter to help with drafting the letters by highlighting the address, date, layout, starting and finishing phrases.

Discussion

Talk to the children about the names of different metals such as iron, steel, aluminium, silver, gold and so on. If possible, link these metals to objects they are made into such as gold into chains, stainless steel into sinks and so on. Discuss with the children the need for addresses. Look at the different elements of an address and what use they have. Encourage the children to use this knowledge to write an address for the robot, such as:

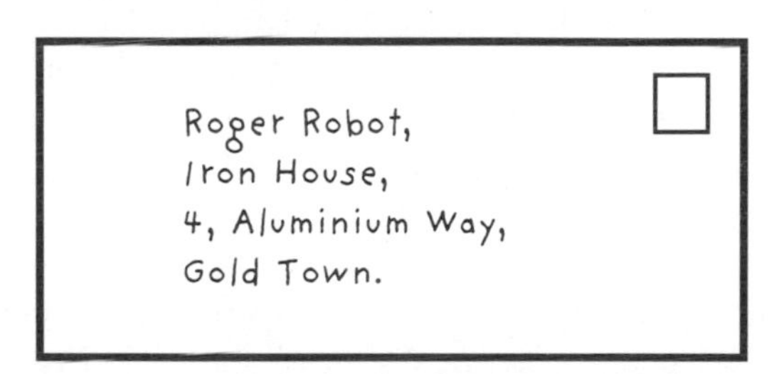

Ask questions such as: Why do letters need stamps? Why are some stamps more expensive than others? How do you know a stamp has been used? How do letters arrive at different places and countries? Who sorts and delivers letters?

Follow-up activities

✧ Contact a different school and establish 'pen friends' for the children to write letters to.
✧ Continue the letters from the robot.
✧ Visit a Post Office or invite a post worker to talk to the children.

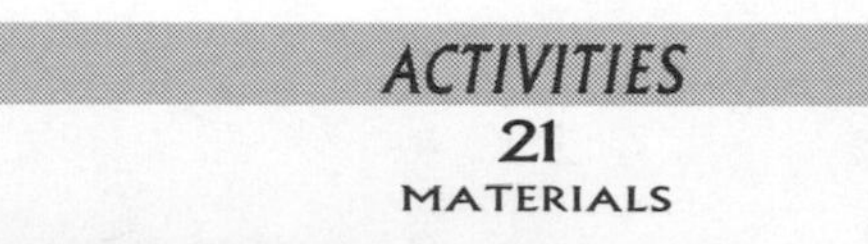

BOOM BANG A BANG!

Objectives

Music – To recognize different musical elements; to compose and perform pieces of music.

Group size

Small or large groups.

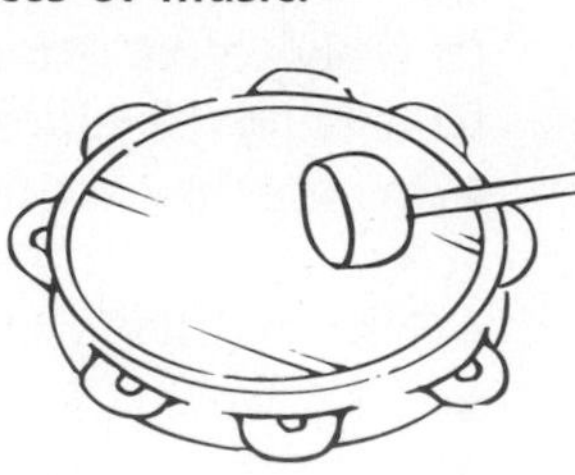

What you need

Selection of nuts, bolts and screws. Musical instruments made from metal (chime bars, tambourines, cymbals, triangles, bells), a range of beaters, metal and plastic trays.

Preparation

Divide the nuts, bolts and screws between the plastic and metal trays. Ensure the children are closely supervised and take care when using small pieces with them.

What to do

Ask the children to close their eyes tight and listen to the noises made by both the plastic and metal tray. Ask them to guess if they are the same and if they know what is creating the noise. Provide opportunities for the children to experiment with these emphasizing pitch, duration and dynamics. Challenge the children to determine what the noise is made from (metal) and see if they can name other metal instruments.

Display the range of metal instruments, choose a child to pick one and demonstrate how it can be played, giving reasons for their choice. Let other children demonstrate other instruments. Once all the children have experienced playing an instrument, focus on them individually discussing:

- How is each instrument played? (Shaken, clashed, hit with hand or beaters – Which is the best beater for each instrument?)
- Describe the sounds they make ('clash' of cymbals, 'ding' of triangle).
- Can the sound be changed or stopped? (By holding the metal.)
- Which instrument makes a long sound?
- Can you make the sound longer? (Using a different beater.)

Following this investigation, distribute the instruments between the children and choose one child to be the conductor. Emphasize to the 'band' that they have to watch carefully and only play their instrument when directed. With the help of the adult and the children working closely together compose and perform a piece of 'metallic music'.

Discussion

Can you make loud noises? Can you make quiet sounds? Can you make long and short sounds? Which sound do you prefer? What do the different sounds remind you of?

Follow-up activities

✧ Devise a story for the children to accompany with their instruments.
✧ Make musical instruments out of metal, such as tin cans, spoons and bottle tops. (Take care when using small, sharp, metallic objects, ensuring the children are supervised at all times.)
✧ Create a musical score to represent their composition:

HOW MUCH IS IT?

Objective

Mathematics – To apply mathematics to real life problems involving money.

Group size

Small groups.

What you need

Selection of 'real money' sorted into containers including 1p, 2p, 5p and 10p coins, variety of small individual sweets, tubs, photocopiable page 91, drawing materials. Selection of 'money cards' each displaying different amounts.

Preparation

Place money and sweets in tubs labelling how much the different sweets cost, and arrange them to enable easy access. Place the set of money cards face down in the middle of the table. Photocopy page 91, one for each child.

What to do

Explain to the children that they are to choose a 'money card' and find the coins to represent the correct amount. Tell them to record this information on the photocopiable sheet. If possible the children should now calculate a different combination for the given amount and again record this.

Challenge the children to 'spend' their money on sweets. They can only spend the given amount, and must suggest different alternatives. If, for example, the child has 10p they can buy five sweets at 2p each or three at 2p and four at 1p each, or two at 3p each, one at 2p and two at 1p each. Stress to the children they must come up with as many ways as possible to 'spend' all their money. Record these combinations on the photocopiable sheets.

Divide out the sweets at the end of the activity and enjoy them together!

Discussion

Ask the children which is their favourite sweets? Why do some cost 3p and some only 1p? How do you buy these small sweets in a shop? Are all the coins the same size and shape? What are the coins made from? What can you see on the coins? Is all money made from metal?

Follow-up activities

✧ Devise task cards for the children introducing the concept of giving change.
✧ Introduce simple multiplication to the children and explain how it can be used when adding up shopping lists.
✧ Encourage the children to role-play being shopkeepers and customers, ensuring they use appropriate language and the correct money.

STICK PEOPLE

Objective

Design and Technology – To discover how materials can be changed.

Group size

Small groups.

What you need

Bundles of thin florist's wire, selection of statues, pictures such as those by Lowry (depicting matchstick figures) and of sculptures (showing people in different poses).

Preparation

Arrange all of the artefacts for the children to examine carefully.

What to do

Look closely together at the pictures of statues, discussing what they are made from. What do they depict? Choose one child to recreate a similar pose as one shown.

Following this, introduce the pictures of the paintings to the children asking them to identify the similarities and differences between the statues and pictures.

Explain to the children they are to create their own figure using the florist's wire. Demonstrate how the wire can be bent to represent arms, legs, feet and so on. At this stage emphasize the hazards involved in using the florist's wire and the need for safety. Introduce a pre-made model to the children, challenging them to use their previously experienced skills of joining, bending and wrapping to make a similar model with the wire.

Discussion

Why is thinner wire easier to work with? What position would the arms and legs need to be in if they were running? Can you make your model balance on one leg? Is the florist's wire pliable? What technique would you use to make the joins stronger?

Follow-up activities

✧ Mould a large wire frame of a figure and cover this with 'Mod-roc' or papier mâché to create a sculpture.
✧ Make a family of wire people complete with wire furniture.
✧ Experiment using different techniques to create a range of wire objects, and add other materials where appropriate, such as a butterfly with tissue paper wings.

SHINY PICTURES

Objectives

Art – To work imaginatively with a range of materials; to develop the use of shape, form and space and evaluate own work.

Group size

Small groups.

What you need

Selection of collage materials including art and plastic straws, lollipop sticks, small reclaimed materials, matchsticks, buttons, twigs, card and so on. Thick card, tin foil, glue, Sellotape, selection of empty metal containers in various shapes and sizes including metal lids, bottle tops, cans and sweet tins. Ensure the children are not exposed to rough or jagged edges by covering any edges with masking tape.

Preparation

Cover the work surface with a protective material and make all the resources available to the children. Cover thick card smoothly with foil. Establish a focal point within the room using the reclaimed metal objects on a shiny metal tray. This could take the form of a scene or an abstract picture.

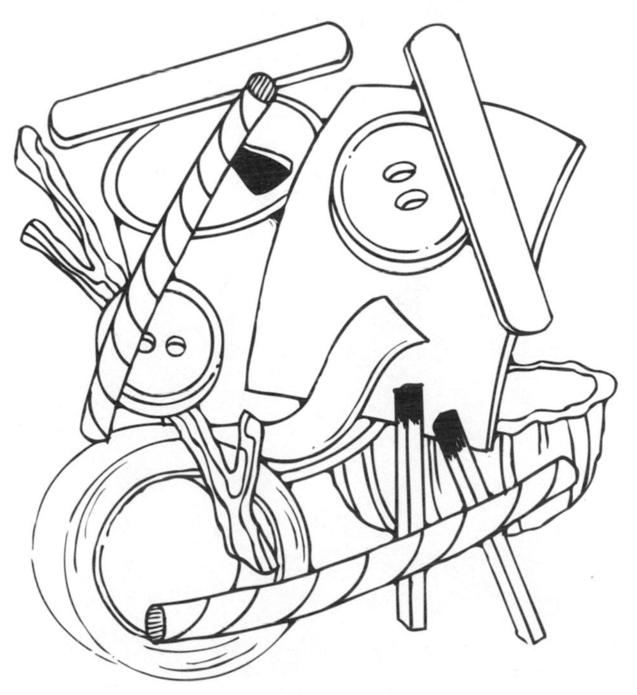

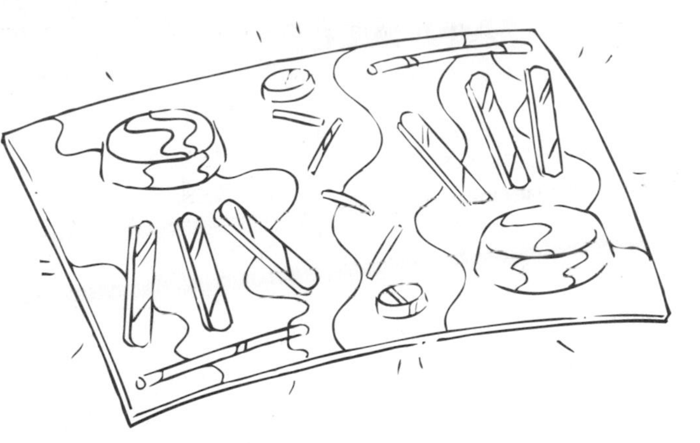

What to do

Invite the children to study the focal point, raising questions such as: What does it look like? Is it all shiny? Can you see a reflection? Can you recognize any shapes? Are all the metal objects the same size? Would you be able to create a similar effect using the resources available?

Challenge the children to decide upon what resources they would use and carefully cover these with metallic foil. Ask them to create a picture by attaching different materials, in an interesting arrangement, onto the covered thick card.

Let the children either create an abstract design or develop a scene. While this is in progress, encourage the children to evaluate and review their work and, if necessary, adapt or improve their ongoing design.

Discussion

Is the foil shiny? Why did we choose to use foil? Is the foil smooth? What happens to foil when it is scrunched? Can you make it smooth again? Will it tear easily? Why does the foil come on a roll and not in sheets? Do both sides of the foil look and feel the same? Does your 'picture' look interesting and why? Would your picture be as interesting if it was flat?

Follow-up activities

✧ Using mosaics as a focal point, develop more intricate designs with smaller collage materials. Once designs are complete spray them with metallic paint.

✧ Make large or individual faces out of metal objects such as paper clips, foil trays, bottle tops and so on.

✧ Make 3D models of robots by covering reclaimed boxes and bottles with tin foil.

TIN CAN ALLEY

Objective

PE – To develop sending and receiving skills using a range of small equipment.

Group size

Any size groups.

What you need

Selection of empty tin cans (ensure all jagged edges are completely covered with masking tape), beanbags, different sized balls, skipping ropes, benches and mats.

Preparation

Prior to this lesson provide plenty of opportunities for the children to practise the following skills: rolling different sized balls, dribbling balls, throwing and aiming beanbags at large and small targets, balancing balls while moving.

Set up a circuit in a large space providing the following stations:

- tin cans evenly spaced and different balls to dribble around them
- tin cans to make a goal and different balls to roll through
- tin cans arranged in piles on a mat, beanbags to aim and throw at the cans and a skipping rope as a marker
- tin cans, balls to balance on top and a bench to walk along.

What to do

As a warm up, encourage the children to travel about the space in a variety of ways taking care not to knock anything over.

Practise skills by choosing children to demonstrate the necessary skills required in each of the 'stations'. For example, dribbling a ball around 'tin can markers', rolling a ball through a 'tin can goal', aiming and throwing a beanbag to rest on top of a tin can and walking along a bench with a ball balanced on top of a tin can.

Now, divide the children into four groups, allocating them a station each. Explain that they are to develop their skills by trying hard at each station until you give a signal to move on. If possible, all groups should experience the four activities.

Afterwards, encourage the children to help put away the equipment.

To cool down, ask the children to imitate a 'tin can' rolling around the space, ensuring they avoid contact with others.

Discussion

Why do we need to warm up or cool down? Why did we place the tin cans on a mat? Could we have used glass bottles instead of tin cans? Why not? Are the tin cans heavy or light? Does this make a difference to the circuit?

Follow-up activities

✧ Consider with the children how they could develop the stations to make them more complex.

✧ Encourage the children to design their own circuit using a range of apparatus.

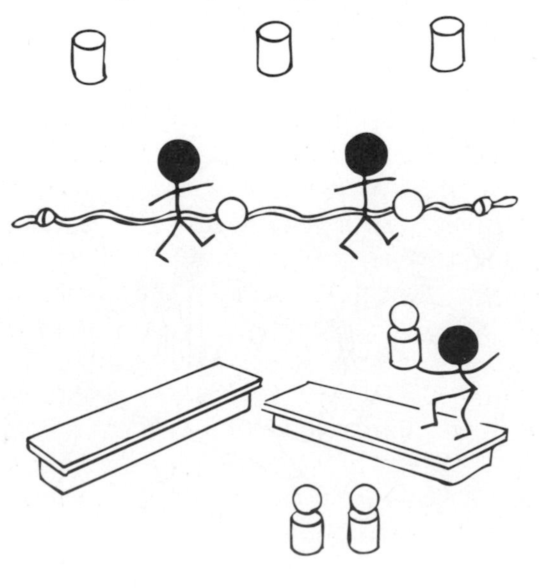

CHAPTER 3 FABRICS

Young children come into contact with many different fabrics every day. This chapter considers the properties of different fabrics and gives children the opportunity to examine repeating patterns and to experiment with colours.

DRIP DROP!

Objective

Science – To investigate the absorbency of different fabrics.

Group size

Small groups.

What you need

Selection of fabrics such as cotton, nylon, corduroy, velvet, felt, polyester, wool and satin, water, magnifying glasses, spoon, plastic covered table or cloth, paper, writing materials.

Preparation

Cut the fabric into similar sized pieces (approximately 15cm × 15cm).

What to do

Allow time for the children to carefully examine the different fabric samples with the magnifying glass. Tell them that if they look carefully through the magnifying glass they will be able to see the threads in the fabric going both along (warp) and down (weft). Discuss with the children the similarities and differences in texture between the fabrics. After some discussion, choose one of the previously discussed properties, such as thickness, and encourage the children to place the fabrics in a simple order such as thick, thicker, thickest. Repeat the process with the other properties.

Tell the children that they will be able to find some of the different fabrics in their own home. Encourage them to suggest things in their kitchen which are made from fabric, such as tea towels, dishcloths, dusters and so on.

Challenge them to guess why all these things are made from similar fabrics. Introduce the word 'absorb', explaining that it means 'to soak up'.

Can the children predict which of the fabrics would make the best dishcloth and why? Ask them to consider a way to determine this, ensuring the test is fair. If the children find difficulty in deciding upon an appropriate test, suggest ideas using spoons and water. For example, they could use a set number of spoonfuls of water for each fabric. Gently lay each cloth on top of the water, then carefully lift up each cloth and decide which one has absorbed most water.

This will be a fair test, enabling the children to discover which fabric is the most absorbent. Once they have completed the experiment, encourage them to record their findings to share with the other groups.

Discussion

Discuss whether the warp and weft are the same in all fabrics. Do some fabrics have wider spaces in between the threads? Are these effective at absorbing water? What is a liquid? Would the results be the same for all liquids? Where does the water go to? How could the water return?

Follow-up activities

✧ Investigate which of the fabrics dries the quickest. Ask the children to consider different methods for drying them.

✧ Experiment with different fabrics to discover which is the best method for drying – wind, sun, radiator and so on. Ensure the children think about the importance of fair testing.

✧ Devise a method for the children to determine which fabric holds the most water, and how it could be measured.

PITTER PATTER!

Objectives

Science – To plan and implement a fair test; to investigate what constitutes an effective waterproofing material.

Group size

Small groups.

What you need

Selection of fabrics including satin, nylon, cotton, velvet, corduroy and so on. Identical plastic containers (approximately 10cm tall), pipettes, water, elastic bands, magnifying glasses, a range of substances with which to 'waterproof' the fabric, for example sticky tape, wax crayons, soap, candles, washing-up liquid and Vaseline, stopwatch or sand timer, writing and drawing materials.

Preparation

Cut several pieces of each fabric slightly larger than the tops of the containers. Make labels to identify the different waterproofing substances.

What to do

Encourage the children to examine the different fabrics using the magnifying glasses, then describe them in detail. Explain to the children that they are going to find out which fabric would make a good raincoat and why. Introduce the word 'waterproof' to the children, explaining that it means 'keeps the water out'.

Challenge the children to complete a fair test. Taking each material in turn, secure the fabric to the container using an elastic band. Decide on the number of drops to be placed on each fabric and the length of time allowed for the liquid to run through. Once the time is up, decide on a way of measuring the amount of water that has dripped through into the container. Encourage the children to record the results in their own way.

Next, discuss how the fabrics could be made waterproof using the labelled substances. Encourage the children to suggest ways they could coat or cover the fabric with the waterproofing substances, such as rubbing the candle over the fabric or sticking on strips of sticky tape. Check the children's hypotheses by testing all the waterproofing materials on one fabric in turn, reiterating the need for a fair test.

After testing each material challenge the children to put the fabrics in order from most waterproof to least waterproof.

Discussion

Ask the children if they have come across any other waterproof materials. What are wellington boots made from? What about umbrellas? What is the opposite to waterproof? What other words can you think of to describe waterproof? Why do we need waterproof things? Would you wear a waterproof swimsuit in the swimming baths?

Follow-up activities

✧ Provide opportunities for the children to experiment keeping objects dry, using plastic bags to waterproof things in the water trough. **(Take care when using plastic bags.)**

✧ Make a waterproof 'roof' for a house made from Lego or Duplo bricks. Encourage the children to test this using a watering can. Does the force of the water affect the results?

✧ Design a pair of waterproof shoes for teddy.

MIX AND MAKE

Objectives

Mathematics – To create a repeating pattern; to name and recognize properties of 2D shapes.

Group size

Small groups.

What you need

Selection of fabric scraps or garments displaying different patterns such as T-shirts, scarves, socks and curtains, a plain item of clothing provided by the children (a T-shirt or vest), fabric crayons, shapes to draw around.

Preparation

Create a display using the range of patterned fabrics, labelling them appropriately.

Write a note to parents asking their child to bring in a plain garment.

What to do

Discuss with the children the different patterns on the fabric scraps, paying close attention to the colours and shapes. Explain to them that a pattern can sometimes be the same basic design repeated at regular intervals, and this is called a repeating or recurring pattern.

Show the children examples of repeating patterns. Ask them to consider their own item of clothing and to think about what patterns they could use to decorate it. Introduce the different shapes, reinforcing the name of each shape and its properties. Provide the children with paper and a selection of shapes, and encourage them to experiment making their own repeating pattern design. Talk to the children about the different patterns they could create such as:

- two colours, one shape
- two colours, two shapes
- three colours, one shape
- three colours, two shapes and so on.

Once the children have finished designing a few patterns, challenge them to reproduce their favourite pattern carefully onto the front of their garment using the fabric crayons and the shapes. Encourage them to design a different pattern on the back of their garment.

Discussion

Ask the children questions to ascertain the extent of their 'shape' knowledge. What is this shape called? How many sides has it got? How many corners has it got? Are all the sides the same? Is the fabric or paper easier to draw on? How does the fabric feel? Does the pattern go across the fabric or down the fabric?

Follow-up activities

✧ Develop the role-play area into a fabric or clothes shop, using the children's decorated clothing.

✧ Weave and tie strips of patterned fabric to create a wall hanging.

✧ Make a family of shape people using different fabrics.

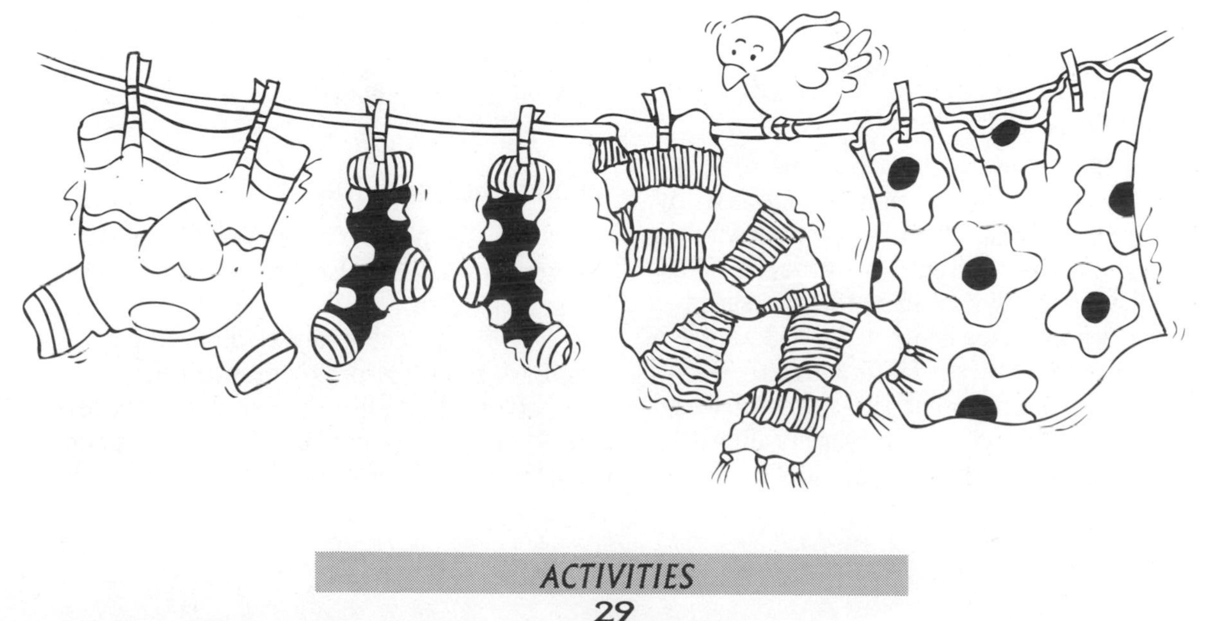

SOCK SWAP!

Objective

English – To extend vocabulary, match words to pictures and work co-operatively playing a game.

Group size

Four children.

What you need

Selection of different types of socks such as long, short, spotted, striped, woollen, coloured, sports and socks with holes in them, all placed in a bag. Several cards depicting socks with similar properties, four baseboards.

Preparation

Make and laminate at least 4 baseboards and 24 sock cards – the same words may be used more than once. Divide each baseboard into six and write on adjectives to describe the socks.

What to do

Challenge the children to choose one sock at a time and describe it, using language such as stripy, spotty, holey, long, short and so on. Talk with the children about the different words they could use to describe the socks, explaining that the adjectives provide a clearer image of what the socks are like. All of them are made from fabric and are socks but they all have particular individual features. Challenge the children to think of and list as many alternative words as possible to describe the socks.

Introduce the sock cards and baseboards to the children, encouraging them to describe each sock and find the appropriate word on the baseboard. If they are struggling with the word, reinforce the strategy of using initial sounds as an aid. Place the cardboard socks face down and invite the children in turn to pick a cardboard sock. If it corresponds to their baseboard they can keep the sock card to cover up the appropriate square on the baseboard, if not they must put it to the bottom of the pile. The winner is the child who has successfully collected six socks.

For younger children, adapt the baseboards to include a picture of the sock and word. Older children may have baseboards and sock cards with more than one property, such as short and striped or long with zigzags.

Discussion

When examining the socks encourage the children to ask questions about the type of fabric, the texture, the weave and so on. Tell the children socks can be hand knitted using wool and three knitting needles. Ask the children if they prefer long or short socks. When and why do they wear socks? What fabric makes comfortable socks? What are two socks called? What else comes in pairs? Do sports people wear coloured socks? Why do we use adjectives?

Follow-up activities

✧ Read the poem 'Patterns' on page 69 of the Resources section. Use it as a stimuli for designing a sock pattern.

✧ Provide the children with a mixed bag of socks and ask them to sort them into pairs.

✧ Let the children make hand puppets using old socks and pieces of felt. Name the puppets and perform a puppet show.

HEXA-FRIEND

Objective

RE – To realize that there are a variety of special people in our lives.

Group size

Any size.

What you need

Photocopiable page 92, a patchwork quilt (if available) or a picture of one, scissors, plain pieces of felt, fabric crayons, sewing materials, magnifying glasses, writing and drawing materials.

Preparation

Cut the felt into regular hexagon shapes. Display the quilt or the picture so that the children can see it clearly. Photocopy page 92, and give one to each child.

What to do

Ask the children if they have a special cover on their bed at home. Explain to the children that some people make their own special quilt covers, which often tell a story or represent a special time in their life.

Show the children the patchwork quilt, asking them to describe what it is made from. Examine the quilt closely with the children using magnifying glasses, discussing how it is kept together, its strength and how the shapes link.

Introduce the photocopiable sheet asking the children to draw themselves in the middle hexagon and the special people in their family in the surrounding hexagons. These are the people who are close to them, who comfort them, who they depend upon and who allow them to feel secure, just like the hexagons on the patchwork quilt are surrounded and linked together.

Explain to the children that there are people outside their own family who are also special. Talk about who these people might be. Why are they special? They may be friends that the children play with or share toys with. Provide the children with fabric crayons and felt hexagons, explaining that they should draw a special time or person on their hexagon. Help the children to stitch the hexagons together to make a class quilt.

Discussion

Ask the children who their best friend is. What do they like to do with their friend? Can they have more than one best friend? What makes a special friend? How do friends make them feel? How do they feel when they break friends? What special times can they remember about their lives? How do people make them feel secure? What else could a patchwork quilt represent?

Follow-up activities

✧ Display the class quilt over a 'bed' with the children's faces under the cover.
✧ Tell the children the story of 'Polly and the patchwork quilt' on page 78.
✧ Teach the children the song 'Hexagons' in the Resources section on page 83.

Use a different shape to tessellate such as a triangle. Is it easier or harder to fit together?

COOL COTTON!

Objective

Geography – To extend knowledge of the children's own surroundings and those of countries beyond their locality.

Group size

Small groups.

What you need

Selection of fabrics including cotton and non-cotton, magnifying glasses, set rings, book entitled *Cotton from seed to cloth* by R Riquier (Moonlight Publishing), a globe.

Preparation

Familiarize the children with the fabrics.

What to do

Encourage the children to sort the fabrics according to their own criteria such as shiny, thick, rough and so on. Choose a cotton fabric, telling the children its name and ask them to re-sort the fabrics into sets of 'cotton' and 'not cotton'. Encourage the children to look closely at the 'cotton' set with the magnifying glass to see if they can find strands of fibres.

Read the information book with the children, allowing them to grasp and visualize the processes involved in making cotton cloth. Explain to the children that cotton garments are usually worn in the summer when it is hot because they are cool to wear. Ask the children if they have been to, or know of, any countries where it is hot, where they would need to wear cotton garments. Ask them to refer back to the book and determine what climate cotton grows in.

Introduce the globe to the children. Talk about what it is, what it shows and how it is used. Together look for the country where they live and one of the hot countries previously discussed. Use the globe to find countries where cotton is grown.

Discussion

Tell the children that cotton is grown in hot countries such as Egypt, Brazil and India. Ask them why cotton is not grown in this country? What colour do they think the cotton plants are? Who picks the cotton? What colour is the cotton? Do all fabrics grow on bushes? Would they like to live in a hot country and be a cotton picker? Do they think the cotton is heavy?

Follow-up activities

✧ Encourage the children to draw and write about the sequence of events outlined above.
✧ Sing the song 'Favourite fabrics' on page 82 of the Resources section, adding noises and actions where appropriate.
✧ Encourage the children to learn the poem 'What are they like?' by John Foster, on page 71 of the Resources section.

SWISH AND SWIRL

Objective

Art – To experiment with colour and textiles.

Group size

Small groups.

What you need

Large pieces of a neutral coloured fabric, string, pegs or elastic bands, cold water dyes, water and bucket.

Preparation

Make up the dye in a bucket following the instructions on the packet.

What to do

Explain to the children that they are going to take their teddies on a picnic. The food and drink are organized but they will need something attractive to lay the picnic on. Ask the children to suggest possible alternatives, prompting them if necessary.

Show the fabric to the children, asking them for ideas to make a bright, colourful cloth. Explain they are going to tie pieces of string tightly around small sections of fabric to make a tie-dye cloth. For younger children, a similar effect can be achieved by using pegs or elastic bands. Ensure the children realize that the area covered by the string will not be coloured/dyed. Once the tying is complete, place the fabric in the bucket of dye, carefully following the manufacturer's instructions. Remove after the suggested time and leave to dry.

Once the fabric is dry, gather the children around. Ask them what they think will have happened to the fabric. Carefully remove the string to reveal the paler circles where the string was tied. Iron the cloth if necessary. You are now ready to begin your picnic!

Discussion

Ask the children to predict what will happen when two coloured dyes, such as red and yellow, are mixed together. Could they make the paler sections square-shaped? Would it make a difference if the string was tied around various objects such as stones, pencils or shells? Talk about the natural dyes that would have been used long ago, such as onion skins or tree bark

Follow-up activities

✧ Design a pattern or create a picture on the fabric using fabric crayons.

✧ Create a batik style picture using a thin flour and water paste to make the outline. When set, paint on the fabric and remove the paste when dry.

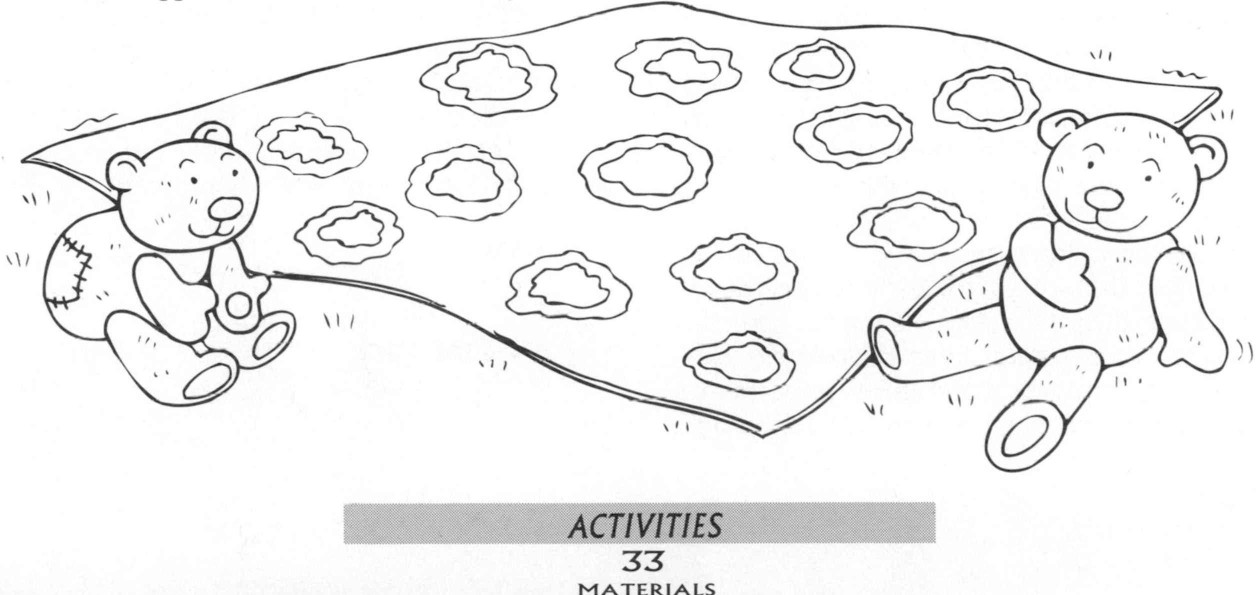

RUB A DUB DUB

Objectives

English – To develop children's speaking and listening skills; to write for a specific purpose considering their audience.

Group size

Small groups.

What you need

The poem 'There's a hole in my pants' by John Foster on page 73 of the Resources section, selection of clothes, bowl, water, washing powder, scrubbing brush, soap, paper, writing and drawing materials.

Preparation

Familiarize the children with the poem. Have warm water readily available and make washing materials accessible. Make the clothes dirty by standing on them or rubbing them in the dirt.

What to do

Recite the poem together with the children asking them to listen carefully for words used to describe the noises made by the machine. Now encourage the children to think of different ways of saying clean and dirty, for example bright, sparkling, scruffy, grubby and so on. Write the words 'clean' and 'dirty' on a whiteboard with the children's suggestions underneath.

Show the children the 'dirty' clothes, asking them how they could make them clean again. Encourage them to think of a way to wash the clothes without using a machine. After some discussion, introduce the washing resources to the children, encouraging them to talk through the process of washing them. Explain that they are going to write a 'rap' together about washing. Start by thinking about the chorus. It could include words such as squelch, swish, swash or splish, splash, splosh.

Challenge the children to sequence the process of washing the clothes in their rap, adding the chorus between each line. A possible example could be:

The clothes are all dirty what do we need?
Splish, splash, splosh,
Splish, splash, splosh.
The water's all hot and the soap is clean.
Splish, splash, splosh,
Splish, splash, splosh.
Let's dunk these clothes in rub a dub dub.
Splish, splash, splosh,
Splish, splash, splosh.
They are so dirty they need a good scrub.
Splish, splash, splosh,
Splish, splash, splosh.

Once complete, encourage the children to perform their 'washing rap' to an audience.

Discussion

Ask the children to describe other sounds made during the washing process. What makes a washing machine work? Why must our hands be dry when switching the machine on or off? How can we dry our clothes? What happens if it is raining? Can all clothes be washed in a washing machine? What would you find at a launderette?

Follow-up activities

✧ Investigate with the children how people used to wash their clothes. Talk about dolly tubs, washboards, mangles and so on.
✧ Encourage the children to identify as many opposites as possible to do with washing, for example hot / cold, wet / dry, clean / dirty and so on.
✧ Teach the children the song 'Rub a dub dub' on page 86 of the Resources section, introducing percussion instruments where appropriate.

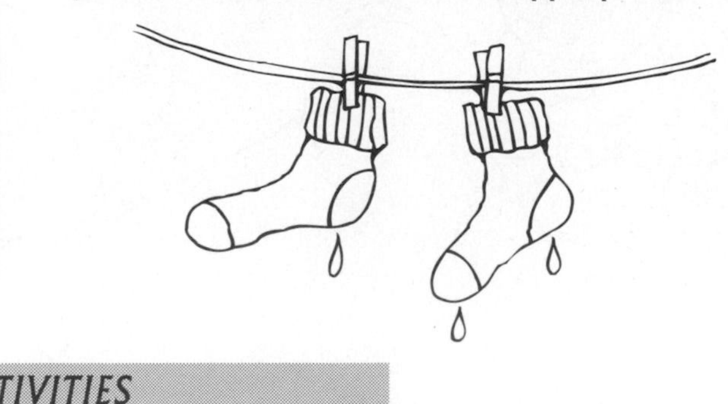

CHAPTER 4
WOOD

This chapter will help children to make the connection between the trees they see around them and the furniture they see in their homes. They will think about the different uses of wood and develop mathematical language as they discover how toys have changed over the years.

ALL IN ORDER

Objective

English – To develop speaking and listening skills and to show a sequence of events through words and pictures.

Group size

Small groups.

What you need

Selection of pictures, picture books and reference books about beavers. Water tray, blue food colouring, branches, twigs, pebbles, bucket full of sand and leaves, writing and drawing materials.

Preparation

Fill the water tray, colour the water blue and submerge the bucket of sand. Stand branches and twigs to represent trees on the edge of the water tray, holding them in place with the pebbles.

What to do

Look at the reference and picture books with the children. Encourage them tó describe the beavers. What is a beaver? What does it look like. Encourage vocabulary such as hairy, brown, pointed, flat, sharp and so on.

Explain to the children that wood is very useful to beavers as it is hard, it floats and the beavers can gnaw and shape it with their strong teeth. Emphasize that a beaver has sharp teeth to gnaw through wooden tree trunks, front paws that look like hands to pull the wood and feet that look like paddles to help push the wood in the water.

Gather the children around the water tray. Discuss with them where the branches come from and what they represent (the forest). Make a model of a beaver dam from the materials, explaining the sequence of events as you build it:

- First the beavers find a suitable position in the river, with lots of trees close by.
- They gnaw down trees and strip them of branches with their sharp teeth.
- They drag the logs to the water with their front paws and place them on mud (represented by sand) and stones to make a dam.
- They use their feet and tails to place more mud on top of the branches to make the dam stronger.

Once the children are happy with this sequence, challenge them to build their own dam in the water tray using the twigs, branches, sand and leaves. When they have completed their dam, encourage them to write down what they have done, and to illustrate the different stages. Challenge the children to add some facts about beavers to their sequence pictures.

Discussion

Tell the children that beavers have sharp, curved, front teeth which never stop growing. The gnawing of the wood ensures they don't grow too long. Ask the children to think of the different sounds the beaver would make, such as splash, crunch, snap and so on. What colour are beavers? Are they large creatures? What is a dam? Why do you think they build dams? Where do beavers live? Have the children heard of the expression 'busy as a beaver'? What does it mean?

Follow-up activities

✧ Encourage the children to make a non-fiction book about beavers, ensuring they include a contents and glossary.
✧ Discover other animals who depend upon trees for their homes.
✧ Challenge the children to create other animal similes, for example slow as a tortoise, cunning as a fox, busy as a bee and so on.

LEAVES AND THINGS

Objectives

Science – To realize differences between living and non-living things; to recognize and name parts of a tree.

Group size

Any size groups.

What you need

Pictures of different trees, selection of leaves and fruit, magnifying glasses, selection of wooden objects, large paper, card, paint, Velcro, writing and drawing materials.

Preparation

If possible, take the children on a walk around a wooded area, collecting leaves and fruits. During your walk, emphasize the shapes, size and variety of trees. Use the card to make labels to name parts of the tree such as trunk, branch, leaves, roots and so on. Draw pictures or gather photographs of different trees on card and label appropriately, for example beech tree, oak tree and so on.

What to do

On returning, discuss with the children the pictures and photographs of trees or talk about the trees they saw on their walk. Make comparisons between the pictures, the children's recollections and a selection of wooden objects, explaining that although the objects are made from trees they are non-living. Carefully examine the leaves and fruit with the magnifying glass, placing similar leaves together. Challenge the children to match the leaves and fruit to the pictures or photographs of the trees.

Paint a large picture of a tree with the group, ensuring they can name each part as it is painted. Include roots, trunk, bark, branches, twigs, leaves, buds, fruit and flowers. When the painting is dry, attach Velcro to the different parts of the tree to correspond with the labels. Challenge the children to pick a name label and attach it to the correct part of the tree.

Discussion

Some trees are coniferous – they do not lose their leaves or change colour throughout the year. Other trees are deciduous – they shed their leaves annually. Ask the children questions about trees. Do all trees have fruit? Are they all the same? What shape are the leaves? What colour are the leaves? Which trees are straight and tall? Which trees are round? Can you wrap your arms around a tree? What is the outer casing of a tree trunk called? Is it rough or smooth? When do the leaves fall off the trees? Do all trees lose their leaves? If not, what are they called?

Follow-up activities

✧ Print tree trunks and leaves with sponges to make a seasons display.
✧ Discuss with the children the similarities and differences between living and non-living things.
✧ Consider processes of other living things.
✧ Read the poem 'Trees' by Brenda Williams on page 72 of the Resources section.

MISS POLLY'S DOLLY

Objective

Art – To explore and use three-dimensional media.

Group size

Small groups.

What you need

Old fashioned wooden 'dolly' clothes pegs, glue, scissors, selection of coloured fabrics, wool and felt-tipped pens. An enlarged copy of the traditional rhyme 'Miss Polly' on page 71.

Preparation

Introduce the wooden pegs to the children, and talk about what they are made from and what they are used for.

What to do

Recite the rhyme 'Miss Polly' with the children, encouraging them to participate in the actions. Explain to the children that they are going to make a special dolly for Miss Polly using the wooden pegs.

On close examination, the children may realize that the top of the peg is flatter, and would ideally represent the doll's head, whereas the rest of the peg is split in two, which would be ideal for the doll's legs.

Challenge the children to use the felt-tipped pens to give their dolly a face, and to glue wool on the peg for her hair. Encourage the children to choose some fabric to dress their doll. If necessary, help them to cut the fabric into appropriate pieces and then let them to attach the pieces to their peg with glue.

Once the dolls are complete say the rhyme again together, using the peg dolls as props.

Discussion

Explain to the children that there are two types of wood – hardwood which comes from leaf shedding or 'deciduous' trees, and softwood which comes from evergreen or 'coniferous' trees. Ask the children which type of wood they think would be easier to carve? Why? What tools could be used to carve the wood?

Ask the children to estimate how many 'dolly' pegs they think could be made from one tree trunk. Ask them to think about other pegs. Are they all made from wood? What other materials are they made from?

Follow-up activities

✧ Read the story 'Little wooden train' on page 74 of the Resources section. Design and make other wooden toys such as dominoes or cars.

✧ Make an extended family of 'peg dolls' to include all generations, which could be used to form the basis of family trees.

✧ Use the peg dolls to dramatize simple stories.

WHAT SIZE?

Objective

Mathematics – To recognize and use the language of measure.

Group size

Any size groups.

What you need

Selection of wooden objects such as blocks, ruler, pencils, twigs and beads, writing and drawing materials, card, photocopiable page 93.

Preparation

Make the wooden objects available for the children to examine and handle. Photocopy page 93, enough for the children to work in pairs. Make size cards displaying the following words – long, short, fat, thin, wide, narrow, tall, small.

What to do

Discuss with the children what is special about all the objects. Can they name other things which are made from wood? Ask them if they know where wood comes from. Challenge them to describe some of its properties such as hard, brown, rough and so on.

Explain to the children that all wood comes from trees. Sometimes it is cut into large pieces (such as planks) and sometimes into small pieces (such as wooden beads). Tell the children how lumberjacks chop down trees in the forest. Ask them if they know what the lumberjacks shout out as the trees fall down to the ground.

Introduce the language of size to the children, explaining the differences between long, short, tall, fat, thin and so on and show the children the size cards. Ask them to choose one of the wooden objects and find two size cards with the most appropriate labels, for example, for a pencil they may select 'tall' and 'thin'. Repeat the process for each object.

Challenge the children to place a set of wooden objects in order of size, for example long, longer, longest. Working in pairs, ask the children to choose one wooden object and size card and locate three other wooden objects in the room to fit the given criteria. For example they could choose a ruler (object) and taller (size card) then suggest a chair, table and door. Record each pair's results on the photocopiable sheet then collate and discuss the results for the whole group.

Discussion

Where are trees cut from? Would all the trees be cut down? Why do we need to plant more trees? Would tall or short trees be chopped down?

Follow-up activities

✧ Using the wooden objects as non-standard units of measure, encourage the children to measure various objects around the room and record the results.

✧ Develop the children's knowledge and experience of non-standard units of measure by introducing them to standard units of measure.

✧ Encourage the children to look outside into the wider environment to discover what other wooden objects they can find outside.

WHO LIVES HERE?

Objective

Geography – To compare different locations and to learn about plans.

Group size

Small groups.

What you need

Globe, pictures of log cabins and tree houses in this country, wooden houses in other countries, such as Sweden and USA. Pictures of animals and birds that live in trees, drawing and writing materials.

Preparation

Discuss with the children which animals build their homes in trees. Show them the animal pictures, asking them to name the different animals. Talk about how and where the animals build their homes and how dependent they are upon trees. Encourage the children to draw pictures of trees including the animals and their homes.

What to do

Explain to the children that it is not always animals that use trees for their homes – sometimes people build 'tree houses'.

Make up a story about a little boy who wanted a tree house, so his dad built a tree house for the little boy to play in with his friends. Make the story as interesting and descriptive as possible.

Challenge the children to plan their own tree house. They will have to make decisions on where the house will be positioned in the tree, how it will be made, what materials they will need, how many rooms it will have, how they will reach it and whether it will need a roof. Encourage them to draw a plan of their tree house and label the various features.

Explain to the children that in this country tree houses are mainly used for children to play in, but in other countries lots of people live in a house made out of wood. Introduce the children to the pictures of the wooden houses, asking them to notice any similarities and differences between these houses and the houses which they live in.

Ask them to suggest which country these wooden houses may be found in. What would the climate be like? Why are the houses built from wood and not brick?

Once the similarities and differences have been noted challenge the children to locate the different countries on the globe.

Discussion

Tell the children how wood can be made into all kinds of different shaped houses, but it has to be painted or varnished to stop it rotting. Discuss with the children why only certain countries have wooden houses. Is it because there are lots of trees in that part of the world? If it rains will the wooden houses leak? What type of trees are the houses made from? Do the trees need to be tall and straight, If so, why? Does it matter when the trees are chopped down? Will there be leaves on them? What else is made from trees? What happens to the part of the tree left underground and what is this part called?

Follow-up activities

✧ Read the poem 'The wooden house' by Jan Pollard on page 72. Encourage the children to write or draw on a tree outline the wooden objects that are referred to in the poem.

✧ Challenge the children to design and make their own log cabin using wooden lollipop sticks stuck together with glue.

✧ Ask the children to consider their local area focusing on the environment, housing, facilities and so on. Challenge them to compare these aspects with a contrasting locality.

FRAMED FRIENDS

Objective

RE – To develop and recognize positive relationships.

Group size

Small groups.

What you need

Selection of plain and ornate wooden frames, thick card, glue, metallic, crêpe and tissue paper, sequins, ribbon, wooden lolly sticks, balsa wood, drawing paper, scissors, magnifying glass, writing and drawing materials.

Preparation

Cut thick card into different sized frames, glue wooden lolly sticks together to make different sized frames and trim drawing paper to fit the frames. Recite the friendship poem 'Patchy bear' by Joan Poulson on page 67. Display the wooden frames so the children can examine, feel and look closely at them with a magnifying glass.

What to do

Introduce the plain and ornate wooden frames to the children, asking what they are made from. Talk about why wood is used. Is it because it is strong or because it can be carved and shaped? Are all wooden frames the same size and thickness? Ask the children why we put pictures in frames. Are all pictures put into a frame? Can other items be framed? Does the style of the picture reflect the chosen frame?

Discuss with the children what makes a good friend, referring to the poem, and scribe the children's suggestions. Choose a child and ask them to describe their friend's qualities without naming the friend. Can the other children guess which friend is being described? Encourage the children to take it in turns to complete this activity.

Next, encourage the children to draw a detailed portrait of their friend, carefully observing each other's features. Explain to the children that they can show other people that their friend is special by placing their portrait in an ornate frame for everyone else to see. Explain to the children that frames are often made from wood, but that their frames will be made from wooden lolly sticks or cardboard. Show the selection of frames to the children and ask them to note any particular features, likes or dislikes.

Provide the children with a lolly stick or cardboard frame and show them the other resources. Demonstrate some of the different effects which can be created using the various materials, then encourage the children to decorate their own frame to enhance their portraits and make them look extra special.

Once the frames are complete, insert the portraits and hang the finished pictures in a 'friends' gallery. Encourage the children to write about their friend, using the letters of their name as a starting point, for example:

P Pick pick pick a friend
A Anybody will not do
U Unselfish, kind and loving too
L Liked by most, but especially you.

Display these next to the framed portraits.

Discussion

Tell the children that a man who works with wood is called a carpenter. In the past, carpenters used special joints instead of nails or screws to join pieces of wood together. These are called dovetail or mitre joints. Encourage the children to look closely at the wooden picture frames. How are the corners joined? What shape is the frame? What is special about the corners? How are the frames hung? Do they stand up? What colour are they? Are all types of wood the same colour? Do they have any patterns engraved on them?

Follow-up activities

✧ Design and make a frame from balsa wood, using card triangles to strengthen the corners.
✧ Use reclaimed pieces of wood such as matchsticks, lolly sticks and pencil sharpenings to make a friendly face picture.
✧ Make a large wooden frame and encourage the children to decorate the edges with their drawings.

TREETOP TRAVELLERS

Objective

PE – To introduce different ways of travelling both on the floor and apparatus.

Group size

Any size.

What you need

Selection of PE apparatus including wooden benches, planks, blocks, mats and agility tables.

Preparation

Explain to the children the need to follow instructions, be aware of safety and use the space effectively. Discuss with the children tree-dwelling creatures and their movements through the trees. Talk about squirrels running up and down trees, monkeys swinging from tree to tree and owls swooping between trees.

What to do

Ask the children to choose one of the tree-dwelling creatures. On a given signal ask the children to move around the space imitating their chosen creature. Do this for a minute or two then let the children to choose another animal and move in a different way when they hear the signal.

Place a different coloured hoop or beanbag in each corner of the room. Instruct the children to move to the given colour using a particular movement, for example swoop like an owl to the yellow corner. Encourage the children to move in different directions such as sideways and backwards.

Encourage the children to set out the apparatus as above. Stress the importance of using the correct procedures for carrying out and maintaining safety aspects. Explain briefly to the children how the different apparatus arrangements can be used, reinforcing the different ways and directions they can move as practised in the floor work.

Zigzag building blocks: Travel on or around the blocks in different ways and directions.
Upturned benches: Travel and balance along the bench or bunny hop from side to side.

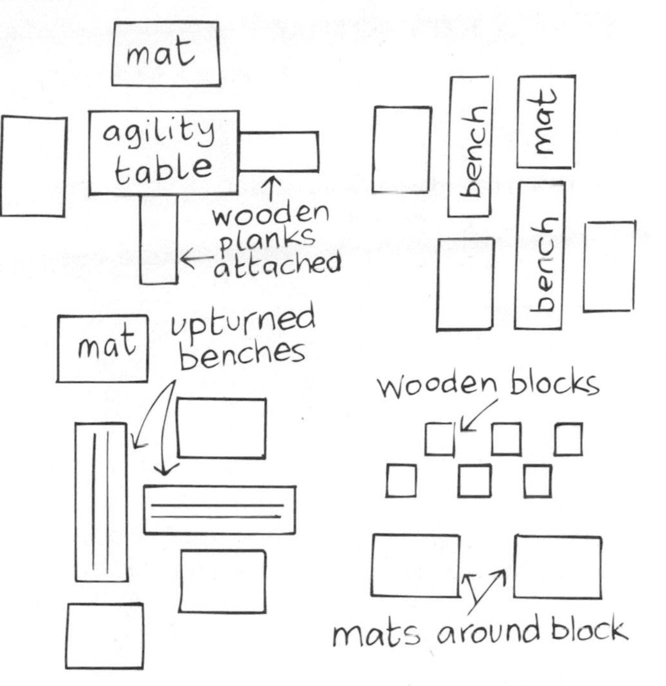

Plank attached to box or agility table: Travel up, down, under and over the plank in a variety of ways. Use different jumps to dismount the box.
Benches: Travel along, over and under the bench or jump on and off using a variety or sequence of movements.

Allow the children time to work on two sets of apparatus then choose some children to demonstrate their movements. Once the apparatus has carefully been put away, ask the children to work on the floor and practise their favoured method of travelling.

Discussion

Ask the children to think about the ways in which different animals move. Are they slow or fast? Do they use two or four feet? Can the children move in a similar way? Do the animals move up, down or along trees?

Follow-up activities

- Continue with the activities through to a second session so all the children have opportunity to work on all sets of apparatus.
- Make sets of cards showing ways to travel, direction and what to travel on. Encourage the children to follow the instructions as they are revealed.
- Design a play area using wooden equipment such as benches, ladders, monkey bars, beams and swinging platforms.

OLD AND NEW

Objective

History – To find out about aspects from the past from a range of sources.

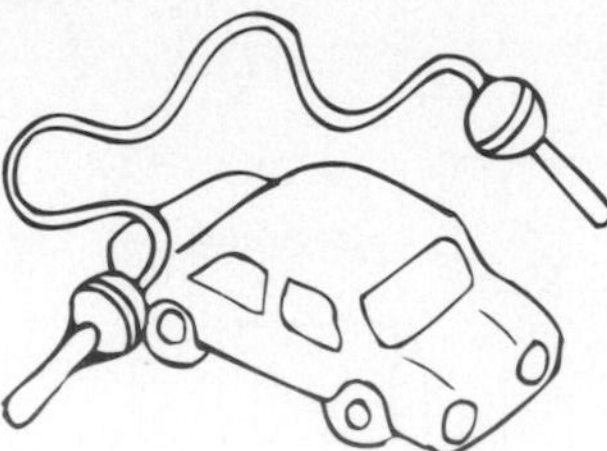

Group size

Small groups.

What you need

Selection of toys past and present including wooden skipping rope, wooden diablo, wooden cup and ball, wooden whip and top (available from most museum shops), doll, toy car, teddy bear, teaset and so on. Sorting hoops, writing and drawing materials.

Preparation

Provide opportunities for the children to play with the toys.

What to do

Ask the children to name their favourite toy and say why they like that one best of all. What it is made from? How do you play with it? ntroduce the present day toys to the children, choosing a child to show how to play with it. Challenge the children to sort the toys into sets using different criteria such as wood / not wood, electrical / non-electrical, moveable / non-moveable.

Show the children the toys from the past and ask them if they would use these toys today. Discuss similarities and differences between the toys, such as:

- Toys from the past were often made from wood, whereas today, modern toys are often made from plastic.
- Toys from the past were not powered by electricity, whereas many modern toys are electric.
- Toys from the past were often simple and unpainted, whereas modern toys are usually bright and colourful.

Ask the children why they think the modern toys are so different from the old fashioned ones. If necessary, prompt with suggestions such as expense – in the past toys were often home-made as people did not have money to spend on luxuries such as toys.

Using the set rings, challenge the children to sort the toys into past and present. If appropriate the children could make a simple timeline using the selection of toys. Now ask the children to make an observational drawing of one toy from the past and one from the present. Make the drawings into a class book.

Discussion

Wealthy families employed nurses to take care of the children. They would often play in a special room known as the nursery where there would be plenty of toys to play with. A particular favourite would be teddy bears, which were named after President Theodore Roosevelt. Ask the children to think of other activities children in the past did. Did the children have gardens to play in? Where else would they play? What type of games would they play in the street? Would the toys break easily? If not, why not?

Follow-up activities

✧ Teach the children circle games such as 'In and out the dusty bluebells'.

✧ Challenge the children to create an individual timeline highlighting key moments in their lives up until the present day and things that may happen in the future.

✧ Tell the children the story of ***The Toymaker*** by Waddell and Milne (Walker Picture Books) carefully considering the pictures and story line.

CHAPTER 5
PLASTICS

Plastic provides a perfect opportunity to introduce the concept of recycling to young children and they will enjoy using the range, shape and size of plastic containers to make early experiences of capacity accessible and fun.

SINK OR SWIM?

Objective

Science – To understand that some plastic containers float and some sink.

Group size

Small groups.

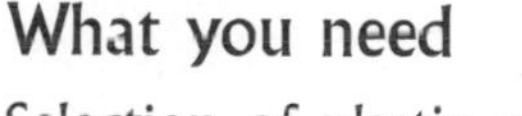

What you need

Selection of plastic containers including shallow and deep containers, bottles with and without lids, polystyrene, plastic bags. **(Take care when using plastic bags. Stress the dangers and ensure the children are supervised.)** Water trough, food colouring, plastic people, string.

Preparation

Fill the water trough with coloured water and make the plastic objects readily accessible. Inflate some of the plastic bags and secure with an elastic band.

What to do

Explain to the children that they are going to rescue their friend who is stranded on an island. They think their friend may have fallen over and hurt their foot. They will need to take medical equipment with them such as bandages, plasters, creams and so on. Pose the children with a problem – tell them they have no boat so they will need to swim to the island, but they must keep the medical equipment dry. Challenge the children to suggest solutions to the problem. Show them the range of plastic objects asking them how they could use the different objects to transport the equipment.

Allow the children time to test their solutions by attaching the objects to the plastic person. Encourage the children to discuss their findings and decide what they should use to help rescue their friend. They will need to consider whether the plastic objects float, whether they are large enough to hold the medicines, whether they let in water and whether they can be easily pulled along.

Ask the children to demonstrate individually how they attached the plastic objects and the plastic figures. Could they suggest any other methods of attaching them together?

Discussion

Ask the children to consider why plastic is a good material to use for this experiment. Is it because it is lighter? More durable? Because it floats? Does a bottle float if it is full of water? What about half full of water? What does it mean when it sinks? Do all heavy things sink? Do all light things float?

Bearing in mind that the island is surrounded by water on all sides, can the children suggest any other ways to reach their friend?

Follow-up activities

✧ Explain other geographical terms to the children such as peninsular, mountain and so on.
✧ Investigate how many marbles a plastic boat will hold before it sinks. Make comparisons between different sized and shaped boats.
✧ Provide the children with a range of different materials and ask them to compare those that float and sink.

WHAT WILL IT DO?

Objective

Science – To sort materials by simple properties and realize that some plastic objects can be changed in shape.

Group size

Small groups.

What you need

Selection of plastic objects which have a range of properties such as hard, squashy, bendy and soft, including bottles, rulers, Lego bricks, combs, tubing, polystyrene, plantpots, straws, bubble wrap, Cellophane and so on.

Sorting rings, two plastic spoons (one previously affected by heat), card, magnifying glasses, writing and drawing materials.

Preparation

Encourage the children to handle and examine the plastic objects.

What to do

Display the objects, asking the children to name any similarities and differences. Choose a child to select an object, and name and label one of its properties. Repeat this until a range of properties have been highlighted such as bendy, squashy, stretchy, scrunchy, hard or soft. Write each property on a piece of card then place one of the property cards into a set ring. Encourage the children to fill the ring with objects that will fit the criteria. Some of the objects may fit into more than one ring, so challenge the children to provide suggestions about how they could overcome this problem. If necessary, overlap the set rings for them and explain that the middle section can contain objects with both properties.

Show the children the plastic spoons, one of which has been affected by heat. Ask them to tell you what is different about the spoons. Why has one changed shape? How did it change shape? Can the spoon be changed back to its original shape again? Tell the children that it is a heating process that initially moulds the plastic to the required shape. Stress the point that heat can make plastic hard or soft.

Discussion

Tell the children that the word plastic means soft, or easy to mould. Why do you think things are made from plastic? What plastics can you scrunch? What is the difference between scrunching and squashing? How can you get rid of plastics? What does recycled mean? Can all plastics be recycled? How could you make plastic different colours? One of the advantages of plastics is that they do not rot or corrode, but this also means they are difficult to destroy and so become a pollution problem. Tell the children that whenever possible, they should recycle their plastic containers.

Follow-up activities

✧ Develop the children's knowledge of recycling. What other materials can be recycled?
✧ Investigate the effect of intense cold on plastic by placing a plastic spoon in a freezer. Is it as bendy as a plastic spoon at room temperature?
✧ Read the poem 'Brand new' by Stevie Ann Wilde on page 70 of the Resources section.
✧ Make 3D models using reclaimed plastics.

FILL IT UP

Objective

Mathematics – To provide opportunity to use purposeful contexts for measuring.

Group size

Small groups.

What you need

Selection of plastic bottles, jugs, plastic cups and containers of various sizes, plastic tubing, funnels, water trough, food colouring, writing and drawing materials.

Preparation

Fill the water trough with coloured water, fill one plastic bottle with coloured water and make other plastic containers readily available.

What to do

Ask the children to imagine that it is a hot day and they are going for a walk. They will need to take a drink with them to cool them down. How will they carry their drink as they are walking? Discuss with the children the different containers they may use such as glass and metal. Encourage them to decide which container would be best based on the weight of the container, for example plastic would be better than glass because it is lighter.

Introduce the filled bottle of 'juice', posing questions such as: We all need a drink, will there be enough in this bottle? How will we find out? What else will we need? Provide opportunities for the children to experiment with the bottles and cups then encourage them to discuss their findings with the rest of the group.

Ask the children to consider what would happen if more people went on the walk. How big would the bottle need to be? Challenge them to estimate and record how many cups each of the other bottles holds. Let them test their estimates and record the results. Once the children have established how many cups each bottle holds, challenge them to order the bottles – from which holds the least up to which holds the most. Explain to the children that they have been using a cup to measure the liquid. As the cups are not always full they may need to consider other ways of measuring liquid. This can be developed into investigating standard units of measure.

Discussion

Ask the children to look at the selection of plastic bottles. Are they all the same? Are they all smooth? Do they have ridges or patterns? Are they light or heavy when full or empty? Can you change their shape when full or empty? If you drop the bottle will it break? Is plastic clear or coloured? Introduce translucent and transparent to the children, explaining that transparent means clear, such as an empty bottle, whereas translucent means the light does not pass through clearly, such as a filled bottle. What other plastic containers carry liquids? What is special about a flask?

Follow-up activities

✧ Fill darkened bottles with a variety of drinks. In turn, blindfold the children and challenge them to taste and guess the drink.

✧ Extend the children's experiences of standard units of measure, considering how different liquids are measured, for example pints of milk, litres of petrol and so on.

✧ Make a bar graph to display the children's favourite drinks.

LOOK AND SEE

Objective

Art – To experiment with mixing colours.

Group size

Small groups.

What you need

A selection of plastic bottles such as washing-up liquid, conditioner, shampoo and tinted bottles, water, red, blue and yellow food colouring, torch, white paper, Blu-Tack, colour paddles or coloured Cellophane and small coloured objects.

Preparation

Fill plastic bottles with coloured water. Attach white paper to a wall.

What to do

Provide the children with colour paddles or coloured Cellophane and encourage them to view their surroundings while looking through the different colours. Talk about their findings. What colours can they see? Do they look the same shape? Does anything remain the same colour?

Provide the children with a red, yellow and blue object asking them to look again through their colour paddles or Cellophane to discover if the objects have changed colour. Are any of the colours lighter or darker? Can you see different shades of colour? Ask them to predict what would happen if they looked through two overlapping colours. Allow time for the children to experiment and test out their hypotheses.

Discuss with the children the selection of plastic bottles, explaining that they are all made from plastic but are different. Can they tell you how the bottles are different? Can you see through them all? Investigate what happens to the water in a tinted bottle. Introduce the plastic bottles filled with coloured water, place these in front of the white paper asking the children to suggest what might happen if a torch is shone through each bottle. Challenge them to discover how they could change the colour reflected onto the white paper. Let them experiment, then ask them to predict what would happen if they placed a coloured block in each bottle of water. Would all the blocks look the same colour? Which colour is the strongest? Does the shade of colour make a difference to the result? Allow some time for the children to experiment, then encourage them to discuss their findings and record the results.

Explain to the children that they are going to use the previous experiences to help them create new colours by dropping small amounts of food colouring into plastic bottles filled with clear water. Challenge them to find out how many colours they can make. How many shades of one colour can they make? What happens if three colours are mixed together? Does shining the torch through the bottle alter the colour? Does it reflect the same or a different colour?

Discussion

Explain to the children that red, yellow and blue are known as primary colours which means you cannot make them from other colours. Green, purple, orange and brown are known as secondary colours which means they can be made by mixing primary colours together. Talk about brightly coloured things such as sweet wrappers. Many sweet wrappers are made from Cellophane, which is hard wearing and tough. Why are some sweet wrappers transparent (see through) and others coloured? Is Cellophane easy to tear? Do the bright colours make the sweets more appealing or is it better to be able to see the sweet? What are the children's favourite sweets? Why?

Follow-up activities

✧ Make coloured binoculars by covering the end of cardboard tubes with coloured Cellophane and sticking two tubes together.

✧ Does the colour of a sweet affect its taste? Encourage the children to work in pairs to guess the colour of a sweet by its taste.

✧ Make a colour wheel with the children and discover what happens when you spin it.

BUILD IT!

Objective

Design and Technology – To design and make a given object using different components.

Group size

Any size groups.

What you need

Selection of plastic construction equipment such as Lego, Duplo, Mobilo and so on. Card, sticky tape, plastic straws, paint, photocopiable page 94, 'Fireman Sam' stories by Rob Lee (Heinemann), model fireman.

Preparation

Familiarize the children with the 'Fireman Sam' stories. Use the card and paint to make a model of a tall tree and a cat.

What to do

Choose one construction kit and carefully consider what it is made from. Explain to the children the function of each different piece, naming the part where appropriate, for example wheels, axles and so on. Demonstrate with the children how each part works, how they can be joined and the different ways they can be used.

Allow time for the children to familiarize themselves with the construction kit and its capabilities. Explain to the children that construction kits are generally made by moulding plastic to achieve the desired shape, such as bricks for Lego. Ask the children what would happen if they dropped their plastic bricks on the floor. How strong is the plastic?

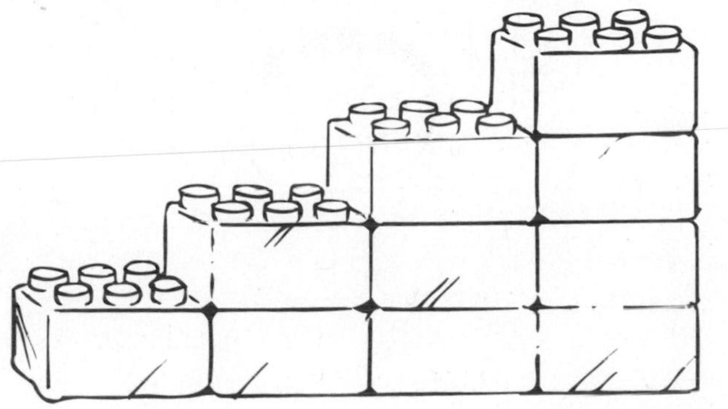

Read stories about Fireman Sam and explain that one of his adventures was to rescue a cat who was stuck up a tree. Show the children the model fireman and the cat and tree made from card. Place the cat at the top of the tree and discuss with the children how the model fireman could rescue it. What would he need to use? Ask questions such as: How tall would the ladder need to be? How many wheels does a fire-engine need? How big would the fire-engine need to be to carry the fireman and the ladders? What else would you find on a fire-engine that you could use to help you rescue the cat?

Challenge the children to work in pairs to make a fire-engine using the plastic construction equipment, card, straws and sticky tape. The model should be able to carry the fireman and his ladders. Remind the children to pay particular attention to the size of the fireman and the tree, and to think about safety.

Once the children have made their model, encourage them to complete the photocopiable sheet on page 94. Challenge them to test out their fire-engine and evaluate with the rest of the group which model would be the best for helping the fireman to rescue the cat.

Discussion

A lot of toys are made from plastic as it can stand up to being knocked about. Why are construction kits not made from glass? Could you make one large fire-engine to carry ten model firemen? How could you make the ladders extend?

Follow-up activities

✧ Develop the children's skills and concepts in modelling by challenging them to copy a pre-made model.
✧ Make a vehicle using a plastic construction kit to carry letters for Postman Pat. Make sure there is room for Jess to ride with him!
✧ Use construction equipment models to supplement other stories or nursery rhymes such as a bridge for the Three Billy Goats.

MORE OR LESS

Objective

Mathematics – To recognize and order numbers to 10 and to understand the concept of more or less.

Group size

Groups of four.

What you need

Selection of plastic objects such as teddies, trees and cubes, small, clear plastic bags, (**ensure safety when using plastic bags**) elastic bands, string, pegs, card, sticky labels, writing and drawing materials.

Preparation

Fill and seal each bag with a different number of plastic objects. Use the card to make number cards 0–10. Make a washing line by attaching string to two chairs, label one end 0 and the other end 10.

What to do

Explain to the children that the bags have been filled with plastic objects and they have to guess how many are in each bag. Encourage the children to place the plastic bags in the correct order along a table, with a number card to show their guesses. Allow them time to check their guesses by opening the bags and counting the objects.

Discuss with the children how they arrived at their initial guess and how could they be more accurate. Once the correct number has been established, encourage them to reseal and number the plastic bags using sticky labels or card tied on with the string.

Introduce the washing line to the children and peg a number card to it. Tell them that when they choose a plastic bag this time, they have to look at its label and decide whether it is more or less than the number pegged on the line. For example, number 3 is pegged on the line, a child then chooses a bag labelled 5, so they must peg it after the number card.

Repeat the process until all the plastic bags are pegged on the line. Start with a different number card each time.

Discussion

Ask the children to suggest reasons why plastic has been chosen for the bags and objects. Is it because plastic bags are strong but light? Is it because you can see through them to count the objects? Is it because they are just the right size? Will the plastic objects break if they fall from the line? Will the bag tear with light plastic objects or heavy wooden objects? Can plastic be cleaned? How is the plastic made into different shapes? Discuss with the children what more or less means, and how they make comparisons.

Follow-up activities

- Introduce balance scales to the children and encourage them to place plastic bags on the washing line using the criteria heavier and lighter.
- Challenge the children to peg and number plastic bags on the washing line which increase in twos or fives.
- Introduce the concept of odd and even numbers.

THE TREASURE CHEST

Objective

History – To recognize changes in children's own lifetime, using a range of sources for information.

Group size

Small groups.

What you need

Selection of household objects from the past such as a metal kettle, flat iron, pottery bowl, glass jug and so on, modern equivalents made from plastic, card, paint, large cardboard boxes.

Preparation

Make a 'treasure chest' complete with lid from a large cardboard box. Paint the box to resemble an old chest.

What to do

Show the chest to the children, explaining that it has been found in a dusty old attic. Build up the suspense by asking them to predict what it will contain, before raising the lid of the box. Choose one of the old-fashioned items and ask the children to guess who it might have belonged to. Why they would use it? When they would use it?

Repeat with the other old-fashioned items. If necessary draw from the children that all these items are from the past.

Encourage the children to handle and examine the objects in order to determine what they are made from. How heavy are they? Ask the children if they think these are the best materials to use or whether they think there is a material used nowadays which is better.

Explain to the children that all of these objects were used a long time ago. How has the design of the objects changed over time? Show the children the plastic objects asking similar questions. Allow them time to handle and examine both sets of objects, then encourage them to sort the objects into two categories – things used a long time ago and things used today.

Discussion

As this is a discussion-based activity, it is important to encourage the children to work together in the group ensuring they are all involved in the conversation. Ask the children which would be easier to use – the heavy flat iron or the plastic iron? Which kettle would be heaviest when filled with water? Which jug would be less likely to break – the plastic or glass? Which bowl would make more noise when the mixture in it was stirred?

Follow-up activities

✧ Display photographs of the children as babies and drawings of themselves. Challenge the children to match them together.
✧ Help the children to devise a questionnaire asking their parents and grandparents about the different things they remember using when they were younger.
✧ Investigate the changes over time in baby equipment such as plastic for glass.

LOOK WHAT I'VE FOUND!

Objective

Geography – To realize the differences between natural and manufactured products.

Group size

Small groups.

What you need

Selection of natural and manufactured plastic materials including wool, leather, metal objects, cotton fabric, can of car oil, plastic containers, plastic toys, plastic cups, plastic pens and so on, set rings, writing and drawing materials.

Preparation

Display the objects, allowing an opportunity for the children to examine them and sort them into two sets.

What to do

Ask the children to explain how they sorted the objects. What properties did they sort by? Can they think of other ways to sort them? Encourage the children to look at the two sets – one containing natural and one containing manufactured objects. If appropriate, explain to the children that natural resources are things that come from nature such as wool from sheep, wood from forests and leather from cattle. Manufactured resources are things that have to be made including plastic and nylon.

Introduce the can of oil to the children, explaining that oil and plastic are linked together. Ask the children if they know how they are linked. Explain to them that crude oil has been found under the sea. The oil has to be pumped out by oil rigs – huge platforms with large drills. The oil is taken to special places where it is refined and treated to make plastic.

Discussion

Oil has been found in Canada and the United States, South America and Africa. Oil is used for making many different things: detergents, dyes, fertilizers, insecticides, beauty products, scents and medicines. Out of every hundred litres of oil, ten go to make these products. Ask the children to suggest why we need manufactured products. What would happen if we relied on natural products? Who develops such products? How do they extract the oil? What else would you use oil for? Would you find oil in your kitchen? What is it made from? What colour is it?

Tell the children that plastic was invented just over a hundred years ago. What was used before the introduction of plastic? Why is plastic a good material to make things out of?

Follow-up activities

✧ Investigate the oil industry, discuss what life would be like on an oil rig.
✧ Sing the song 'Plastic' on page 85 of the Resources section.
✧ Make a list of plastic things used during the day. Are they hard or soft plastics?
✧ Consider the phrase 'plastic money' and discuss what it means and how it is used.

CHAPTER 6
BUILDING MATERIALS

The structured play activities in this chapter encourage children to think about the range of materials used in buildings and about the people who use them. Children are made aware of the possible hazards of building sites and there is an emphasis on safety.

THIS LITTLE PIGGY

Objective

Science – To investigate materials through a fair test.

Group size

Small groups

What you need

A copy of the song 'The big bad wolf' by Ann Bryant on page 88 of the Resources section, plastic pigs, twigs, straw, plastic building bricks, string, sticky tape, masking tape, glue, hairdryer, writing and drawing materials.

Preparation

Teach the children the song about the three little pigs and their homes. Prepare a chart to collate the results of the investigations (below). Ensure there is access to a power point and outline the dangers of children touching power points.

What to do

Introduce the different materials and ask the children to talk about them. Which material would be most suitable for making a house for the pigs?

Challenge the children to work in pairs to design and build a strong house from straw, sticks or building bricks. Let them experiment with different ways to secure the materials using the glue, tape or string. Tell the children that the pigs are inside their homes and that the wolf (a child) is going to try to blow their house down. Challenge the children to predict which house will remain standing and which will 'blow down'. Record the results on the chart with a sad or smiley face to show whether the pigs escaped from the wolf or not.

Talk about the way in which the houses were blown down. Attempt to draw from the children that each house was not necessarily blown in the same way and challenge them to think of another means of blowing the houses down.

Introduce the hairdryer, suggesting this would be a fairer way of blowing the houses down. Carry out the test again using the hairdryer and record the results.

Discussion

Why could the wolf not blow down the brick house? Explain to the children that house bricks are made from clay which is dried and baked in a very hot oven to make it hard. Why are houses made from bricks? Have the children ever seen a straw house? Which pig was the most sensible?

Follow-up activities

✧ Find some bricks and brick patterns in the local environment. Are they all the same?

✧ Make brick rubbings, challenging the children to discover where they have been taken.

✧ Ask the children to consider the different uses of the other materials – where would you find them? What use do they have?

HUNGRY HOUSE!

Objective

Design and Technology – To realize that materials can be changed to suit different purposes.

Group size

Small groups.

What you need

Large square cake tin, 250g self raising flour, four eggs, 250g margarine, 250g caster sugar, mixer, bowl, knife, oven, greaseproof paper, cake board, red food colouring. *To decorate:* 200g margarine and 375g sieved icing sugar (for butter cream), a range of sweets in different shapes and sizes such as chocolate drops, liquorice, chocolate mint sticks, mini chocolate rolls, chocolate mint squares and marshmallows.

Preparation

Set the oven to 180°C, grease and line the cake tin. Cream the margarine and sugar to make butter cream and put in a few drops of red food colouring. Cover the work surface and place sweets in dishes. **Ensure the children are made aware of safety and hygiene procedures and check with parents for food allergies.**

What to do

Make a sponge cake by creaming the margarine and caster sugar together. Add the eggs and mix, then sieve in the flour and stir. Place the mixture in a prepared baking tin and cook for 30 minutes or until golden brown and springy. Remove from the oven and place on a wire cooling rack.

Meanwhile, familiarize the children with the story of Hansel and Gretel. Explain to the children they are going to make a Witch's Cottage using the cake and sweets.

Once the sponge is cool, place it on a cake board and cover the surface with butter cream. Discuss with the children how they might represent the different features of the house using the sweets, emphasizing the shape, colour and texture of the building materials. If necessary, prompt them with suggestions to use the chocolate mint squares for windows, mini chocolate rolls for the chimney pots, mint sticks for window frames and marshmallows for the roof. Encourage the children to take turns to each add a feature to the house.

Once the cake is complete, recap on the story and encourage the children to take on different roles and act out the story. When they reach the appropriate part of the story, let the children playing Hansel and Gretel eat a named part of the house before sharing the cake out among the rest of the children.

Discussion

Talk about the different shapes and sizes of various types of houses. Are all roofs the same shape? What are real roofs made out of? Do any of the children live in high-rise houses or bungalows? What shape are the windows in their house? Are all windows square? Where might they find round or rectangular windows?

Follow-up activities

✧ Design and build a small town using reclaimed materials. Include a block of flats, a church, shops and houses.

✧ Encourage the children to make simple models of their own houses using construction kits. Position them together to form a street.

✧ Tell the story of the 'The newspaper princess' by Jackie Andrews on page 76 of the Resources section. Challenge the children to design their own fancy dress costume.

BUILDING LIST

Objective

English – To write a list in response to a given stimuli.

Group size

Small groups.

What you need

Selection of pictures from magazines depicting interiors and exteriors of different houses, sugar paper, copy of the poem 'Playdough people' by Tony Mitton on page 68 of the Resources section, photocopiable page 95, writing and drawing materials.

Preparation

Photocopy page 95 and give one copy to each child. Familiarize the children with the poem. Cut and mount the magazine pictures on sugar paper.

What to do

Introduce the photocopiable sheet and various pictures to the children. Explain that they are going to examine the pictures and then make a list of the different building materials that they would need to build a home for some 'playdough people'. Talk about the different shapes, colours and materials in the pictures and encourage the children to write these down on their photocopiable sheet.

Encourage the children to work independently using their sounds knowledge to spell the different materials. Once they have completed their list, challenge the children to draw a house for the 'playdough people', incorporating the different features they have noted.

Discussion

Explain to the children that underneath all buildings are foundations. These are built first. Do the children know why foundations are needed? What would happen if the foundations of a house crumbled? What materials are used to build the foundations? Do they have to be strong? Talk about other things that can be seen as a house is built. Have the children ever seen scaffolding? Why do they think it is used? What is scaffolding made from?

Follow-up activities

✧ Compare electrical appliances found in a kitchen and bathroom, emphasizing the need for safety in these rooms.
✧ Read the poem 'Materials' by Trevor Harvey in the Resources section on page 67. Challenge the children to compose their own poem relating building materials to their uses.
✧ Encourage the children to make lists of describing words for each of the building materials. Use the poem 'What are they like?' by John Foster in the Resources section on page 71 as a stimulus.

CEMENT IT!

Objective

Design and Technology – To design and make a 'brick'.

Group size

Small groups.

What you need

Selection of house bricks showing different colours and patterns, self-drying clay, paint, glue, selection of found objects such as fir cones, straws, blocks and so on, plastic table cloth, wooden boards, blunt knife and other Plasticine tools.

Preparation

Cover the work surface and slice the clay into manageable pieces. Make a glaze using thick glue and water.

What to do

Show the children the selection of house bricks and ask them to think about what they are made from. Are they all the same? How do they feel? Are there any patterns on them? Explain to the children that the bricks are made from clay similar to the piece of clay they are going to work with. Provide each child with a piece of clay and encourage them to work it into a brick (cuboid) shape. Tell the children that they are going to design and create their own brick patterns similar to those they have seen on the house bricks. Provide them with the found objects and let them experiment pressing the objects into the clay to make their own patterns. As they proceed, encourage the children to evaluate their 'brick', thinking of ways to enhance the pattern. Could they make a repeating pattern? What about a diagonal pattern?

Once the bricks are dry, let the children paint and glaze them. Display the bricks by stacking them to make a wall. Add descriptive suggestions from the children such as 'bright, brilliant, busy, brick wall'.

Discussion

Tell the children that bricks are regular shaped blocks of clay, which are left to dry and then fired in a very hot kiln. In the past, bricks used to be moulded by hand and still are in some countries such as India and Malawi. Explain that a bricklayer uses a spirit level and plumbline to make sure the wall is straight. Why do walls need to be straight? Why are the bricks not laid directly on top of each other? What else is made from bricks?

Follow-up activities

✧ Use the clay to make ornaments such as coil pots or animals.

✧ Look closely at examples of stained glass windows. Challenge the children to design and make their own stained glass windows using coloured cellophane and black sugar paper.

✧ Invite a bricklayer to come into school to demonstrate to the children how and what they use for laying bricks.

NAME THAT JOB

Objective

Design and Technology – To name and realize that workers use specialized tools and materials.

Group size

Any size groups.

What you need

A copy of the poem 'Build a house with bricks' by Brenda Williams in the Resources section on page 71. Card, writing and drawing materials.

A selection of resources related to five or six specific jobs in the building trade, for example, plugs, screwdriver and wire for an electrician; metal piping, spanner and tap for a plumber; hard hats for all site workers.

Preparation

Make a table-top display, grouping the resources for each trade together. Allow the children time to handle them with care ensuring they are aware of safety issues. Read 'Build a house with bricks' by Brenda Williams and discuss with the children the different tradespeople mentioned.

What to do

Explain to the children that all houses are built from a range of different building materials. Encourage them to think about and to name some of the materials using the display to help. As the children name each material add the appropriate label to the display. Ask the children how many people or workers they think it would take to build a house.

Encourage the children to look closely at the items on display. Ask them what each material or object is called. What do they think the materials and objects are used for? Do the children have any of these objects in their own homes?

After some discussion, the children should begin to realize that a range of trades, skills and materials are used to construct a house.

Discussion

Why do people on building sites wear hard hats? Do all the workers work outside? When does the plumber, electrician or plasterer start work on the house? What other jobs need to be carried out before a house can be lived in? Prompt the children with suggestions of decorating, fitting appliances, carpet laying and so on.

Follow-up activities

✧ Mime each of the different jobs and challenge the rest of the group to guess, then in a group, role-play different tradespeople building a house.
✧ Talk about the unusual places that some people live such as windmills, barges and so on.
✧ Write letters to invite a tradesperson in to demonstrate a little of what they do and speak to the children.

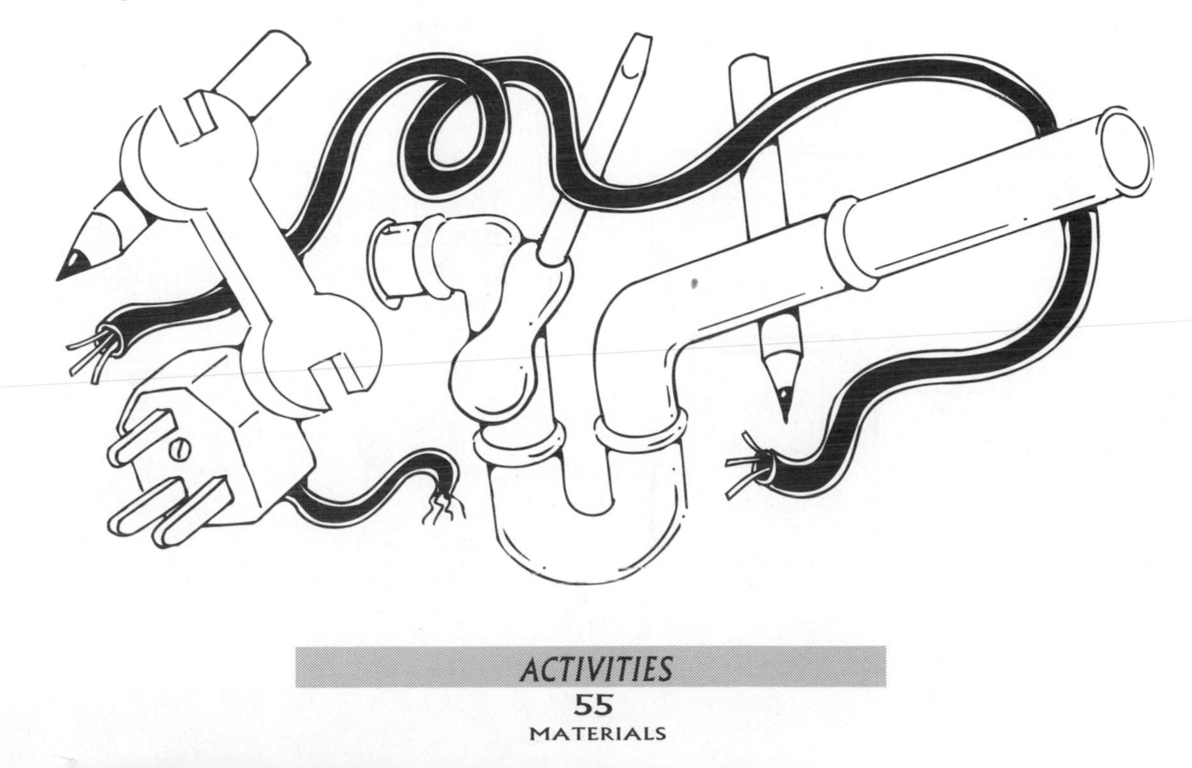

SPIN AND FIND

Objective

Mathematics – To consolidate and apply rules of addition.

Group size

Groups of four.

What you need

Red, brown and blue coloured card, spinner, drawing and writing materials.

Preparation

Follow the diagram below to make four baseboards in the shape of a house, and four sets each of:

- six 'bricks' in red card labelled with number bonds to 7, 8, 9 and 10
- two 'windows' in brown card labelled with number bonds to 6
- one 'door' in blue card labelled with a number bond to 5.

Ensure the sets show a range of number bonds.

Make a spinner by dividing a hexagon into six triangles and numbering them 5–10. Attach to thin card and secure a cocktail stick or a matchstick in the centre.

What to do

Talk about the baseboards with the children, asking them what each section of the house is called and what material it is made from. Encourage the children to state the specific properties of each of the building materials, for example, glass is used for windows because it lets the light shine through; bricks are used to build the house because they are strong and hard wearing.

Explain to the children how to play the game. Each player chooses a baseboard, 6 bricks, 2 windows and 1 door. Each player in turn spins the spinner to discover which number bond they can place on their baseboard. The number bond on the brick, window or door has to match the answer on the spinner, for example if the spinner shows 8, the child can place a brick displaying '6 + 2 =' on the baseboard. Once they have had their turn they pass the spinner on to the next player. The winner is the first player to complete the house.

Discussion

Tell the children that the glass in windows is made by mixing sand and other things (limestone and chemicals) in a hot furnace. Glass is ideal for windows because it is transparent – we can see through it – and it keeps out the rain and wind. Discuss with the children what else is made from glass. Is all glass transparent? Where would you find coloured glass? What is special about the glass in windscreens? Are mirrors made from glass?

Follow-up activities

✧ Teach the children the song 'Building' by Johanne Levy found in the Resources section on page 81, introducing percussion as appropriate.

✧ Make a graph to represent the colour of children's front doors or number of windows on the front of their house.

✧ Attempt to develop the house building game further by introducing subtraction, missing numbers and so on.

THE CONSTRUCTION SITE

Objective

English – To plan and develop opportunities for speaking and listening.

Group size

Small groups.

What you need

Selection of hard hats, wooden building blocks, workers' plastic tools such as trowel, hammer, saw, screwdriver, nails, spanner, spade, wheelbarrow and so on, toy telephone, plastic money, envelopes for wage packets, sticky tape, book for ledger, list of supplies and suppliers' telephone numbers, ***Building Site*** by Carol Watson 'Busy Places' series (Franklin Watts), writing and drawing materials.

Preparation

Show the children the book ***Building Site*** by Carol Watson, which shows the processes involved in building a house. Encourage the children to identify the different people who are shown on each page.

What to do

Challenge the children to build a house using the building blocks and workers' tools. As they work, encourage them to describe each process in detail. Discuss with the children how they could convert their role-play area into a building site. Encourage discussion about the different workers on the building site such as bricklayers and carpenters, the different tools the workers would need such as trowels, hammers and nails, and the clothes the workers would need to wear to keep them safe and protected such as overalls and hard hats.

Once the children are happy with some of the different jobs and equipment, arrange and equip the role-play area with suitable substitutes.

Explain to the children that on each building site there is a foreman who helps to oganize the work and workers. Some of his work takes place in a site office. Here the foreman needs to keep a record of the names of the workers, their jobs and how much they are paid; the building materials they need to order and the supplier details; details of jobs still to be completed and details of colour schemes for the buildings.

Arrange a place within the 'building site' where the site office could be positioned and resourced. Once the 'building site' is complete allow opportunities for the children to take on the different roles within it.

Discussion

Tell the children that before a building is started the land on which it will be built must be measured and surveyed. The surveyor uses tape measures and a theodolite (an instrument which measures angles) to produce a site plan. The architect looks at the site plan and designs the building making detailed drawings.

As this activity focuses on developing the children's speaking and listening skills, encourage them all to participate and to value the opinion of other people.

Follow-up activities

✧ Encourage the children to become architects and draw up their own detailed pictures of buildings. Ask them to describe features of their building to the rest of the group.

✧ Use the song '1, 2, 3, 4 Ev'rybody play' by Jean Gilbert on page 80 of the Resources section, substituting different workers on the building site, for example listen to our hammering sounds bang, bang, bang.

✧ Challenge the children to discuss and demonstrate different verbs (action words) which may be used on a building site.

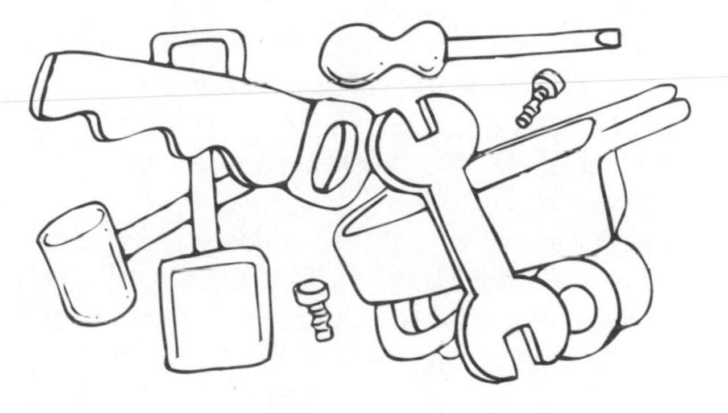

LOOK OUT!

Objective

English – To be able to write for a specific purpose. To identify that pictures are an aid when reading. To develop skills in speaking and listening.

Group size

Small groups.

What you need

Work clothes, hard hats and workman's tools from a construction kit, paper, writing and drawing materials, card, sticky-backed plastic.

Preparation

If possible, invite a construction worker or local builder to talk to the children about the hazards and dangers on a building site. If this is not possible, show the children pictures, books or videos of work on a building site.

In an open space, set up a building site scenario posing different dangers, for example, slippery underfoot, falling masonry, hazardous tools, fenced off areas and so on.

What to do

Dress up some of the children as construction workers, encouraging them to act out the given scenario. Talk about how the workers are informed of the dangers on the building site. If necessary, prompt the children by suggesting notices or brightly-coloured tape.

Make the writing and drawing materials available and challenge the children to design an appropriate poster warning people of the different dangers on a building site. Encourage the children to draw clear, relevant pictures to enhance their posters. Let them write, or scribe for them, the word 'Danger!' together with any other appropriate text they would like to include.

Discussion

Ask the children what colours they associate with danger. How many posters will they need to make? Where should the posters be positioned on the building site? How could they make their posters more noticeable? What do construction workers do? What are the different tools called?

Follow-up activities

✧ Let the children make a model building site with using reclaimed materials.

✧ In turn, encourage the children to mime jobs done on a building site. Challenge the others to guess what it is.

✧ Use the sand tray to create a building site with gravel and diggers. Pose different problems for the children to solve, such as moving piles of sand around and so on.

CHAPTER 7
DISPLAYS

Displays are invaluable in creating an interesting environment, extending learning opportunities for children and allowing teaching points to be developed. This chapter offers four display ideas, making use of a range of materials covered in the activity chapters.

Introduction

All children flourish through praise, encouragement and a sense of achievement, and display is the ideal tool to achieve this. It is essential as educators of young children, that we demonstrate the value of their work and as a result develop their self-esteem. Children's imaginations are vivid and colourful, their talents many and varied, and there should be a variety of displays in their environment which reflect this. Displays should represent work from each child, as they all have something to offer. Their contribution may not be perfect but it is important for them to see their work valued and displayed. Displays should communicate ideas, so they should therefore be lively and interesting, grabbing the children's attention and providing a catalyst for discussion with their peers.

To gain the most from displays, a range of techniques and materials should be used. Where appropriate, place displays at children's level to encourage them to interact – developing their vocabulary and powers of observation. Displays could be 2D, 3D and suspended at various heights to add interest. They should create opportunities for completing structured tasks, following instructions and experiencing different textures, such as draped materials, textured papers, corrugated card, plastics and metals.

All displays should be supplemented with large, clear labels and captions completed by both the adult and children. Lettering should take a range of forms and sizes, and like the children's work itself, always mounted or framed on colours which complement each other.

MATERIALS AVENUE

What you need

Coloured backing paper, large squares of stiff card, scissors, stapler, glue, felt-tipped pens.

A selection of different materials including: Wooden: bark, lolly sticks, balsa wood, cork, pencil shavings, matchsticks; Plastic: polystyrene curls, lids, sequins, crisp bags; Metal: paper clips, butterfly clips, coins, milk bottle tops, foil trays; Fabric: woollen, stripy, satin, checked, velvet, seersucker; Paper: tissue, tracing, sugar, cartridge, reclaimed boxes, art straws.

What to do

Cover the display board with brightly-coloured backing paper. Ensure the children are aware of the safety aspects before encouraging them to examine and sort the materials. Organize the children into five small groups and provide each group with a large card square. Tell them that they are going to turn their card squares into different houses using the collage materials. They will be making a wooden house, a plastic house, a metal house, a fabric house and a paper house.

Talk about how they could use the various materials for different parts of their houses. Prompt with ideas if necessary. For example, for the wooden house they could use cork for the chimney pot, lolly sticks for the roof, pencil shavings to represent the pebble dash, balsa wood for the window frames, bark for the path and matchsticks for the door.

Before they begin to collage the materials, encourage the children to draw outlines of the windows, door and roof on their piece of card. Let the children work together to glue the different materials in place on the cardboard. Attach the completed houses to the display board and add a border of different materials around the edge. Label each house according to the materials it is 'built' from.

Discussion

Talk about the various materials with the children. Encourage them to describe how the materials feel and look. Which house do they think is the most attractive? What sort of people do they think might live in the different houses? Which house would be the noisiest to live in? Why? Which would be the most comfortable to live in?

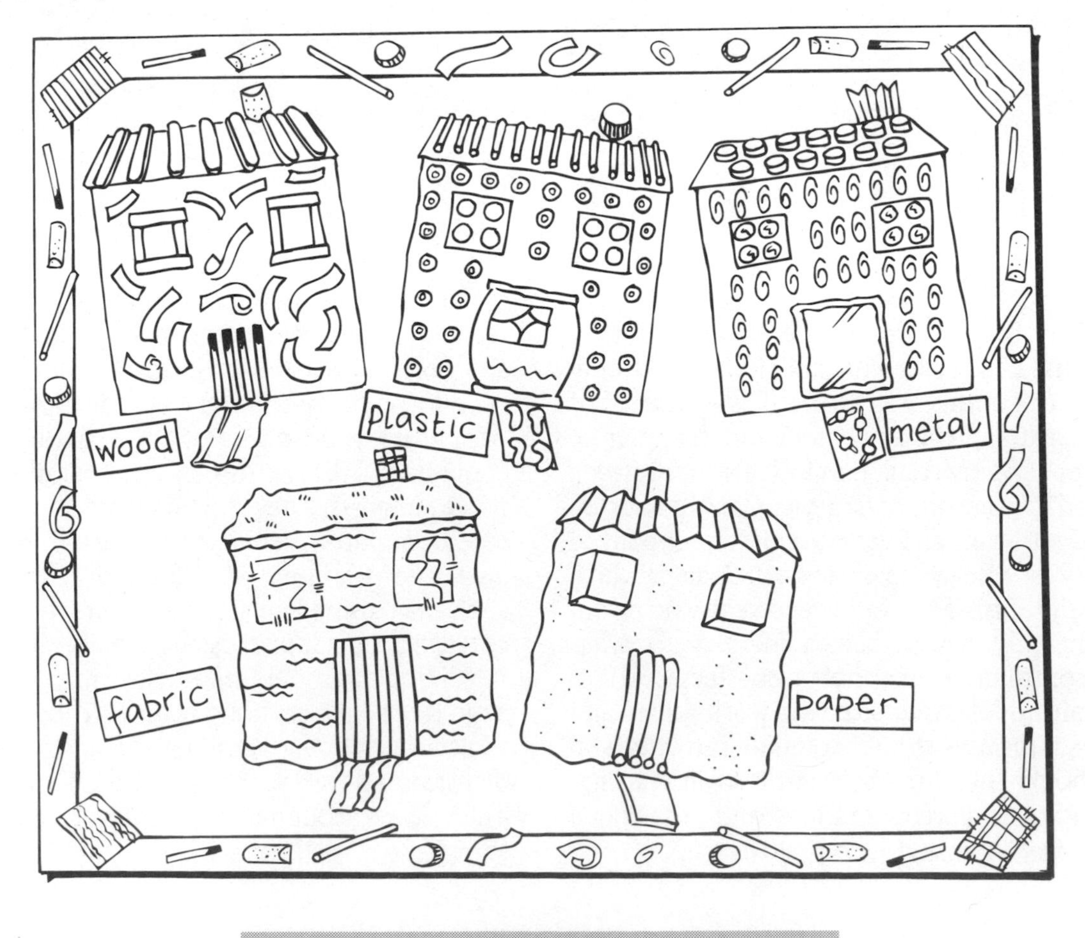

HEH HOH TREASURE!

What you need

Thin card, backing paper, foil paper, white A4 paper, yellow fur fabric, wood shavings or bark, brown and blue Cellophane paper, brown, blue and green paint, sponges, glue, green tissue, polystyrene curls, sequins, assorted fabric, sand tray, pebbles, plastic tub, sticky-backed plastic, comb, scissors, adhesive Velcro, water, red ribbon, stapler, table.

What to do

Create a pale blue sponged pattern on the backing paper to represent the sea. When dry, use to cover the display board. Ask the children to draw an outline of an island on another piece of backing paper and sponge it pale green. Explain to them that they are going to use the collage materials to make individual pictures of each area on the island to make a map. The map will need to include a clump of trees, a winding river, a village, a sandy beach, rocks and a mountain range.

Encourage the children to work in small groups to collage the different areas on the pieces of thin card. Cover the finished pictures with sticky-backed plastic then attach them to the island outline using a strip of sticky tape across the top edge only, so that they can be lifted. Attach a piece of Velcro to the map underneath each picture.

Let the children make a 'treasure chest' on a smaller piece of card and cover it with sequins and foil to represent jewels. Attach a piece of Velcro to the back of the 'treasure chest' so that it can be moved around the map and stuck in different places behind different features.

Place the sand tray on a table in front of the display board. Challenge the children to create a scene with sand dunes, rocks and water. Place pre-made scrolls on the table made from rolls of paper tied with red ribbon. Let the children hide the 'treasure chest' in different areas of the map and make treasure maps on the scrolls for the other children to find it.

Discussion

How would you describe the areas on the island? Would you find pirates on the island? Where might they be? What clothes would they wear? What would they carry? What words could you put on the display? How could you represent a forest or beach on the treasure map?

NATURAL PATTERNS

What you need

Black backing paper, border roll, thin card, coloured paper frames, selection of coloured pictures portraying fish, flowers and animals taken from magazines, coloured foil, coloured gummed paper, coloured fabric, paper, stapler, scissors, glue and spatulas.

Preparation

Cover the display board and mount the pictures. Cut narrow strips of paper and fabric.

What to do

Provide each child with a coloured picture. Explain that they are going to look at their picture and decide what colours and patterns they can see. Give each child a piece of card and challenge them to create a design reflecting the colours and patterns in their picture. Encourage them to think about which material would be most appropriate for each pattern. They could use the fabric strips for flowers, coloured metallic foil for the fish and coloured gummed paper for the animals. While the children complete this activity, reinforce the need to examine their picture frequently and to carefully match the colours.

Once the children have completed their pattern, choose an appropriate coloured frame to mount and display their work.

Discussion

Can you label the materials used? Why did we use shiny metallic paper for the fish? What other materials could we have used? Do the patterns match the pictures? Are the colours warm or cold? Are there different shades of colour?

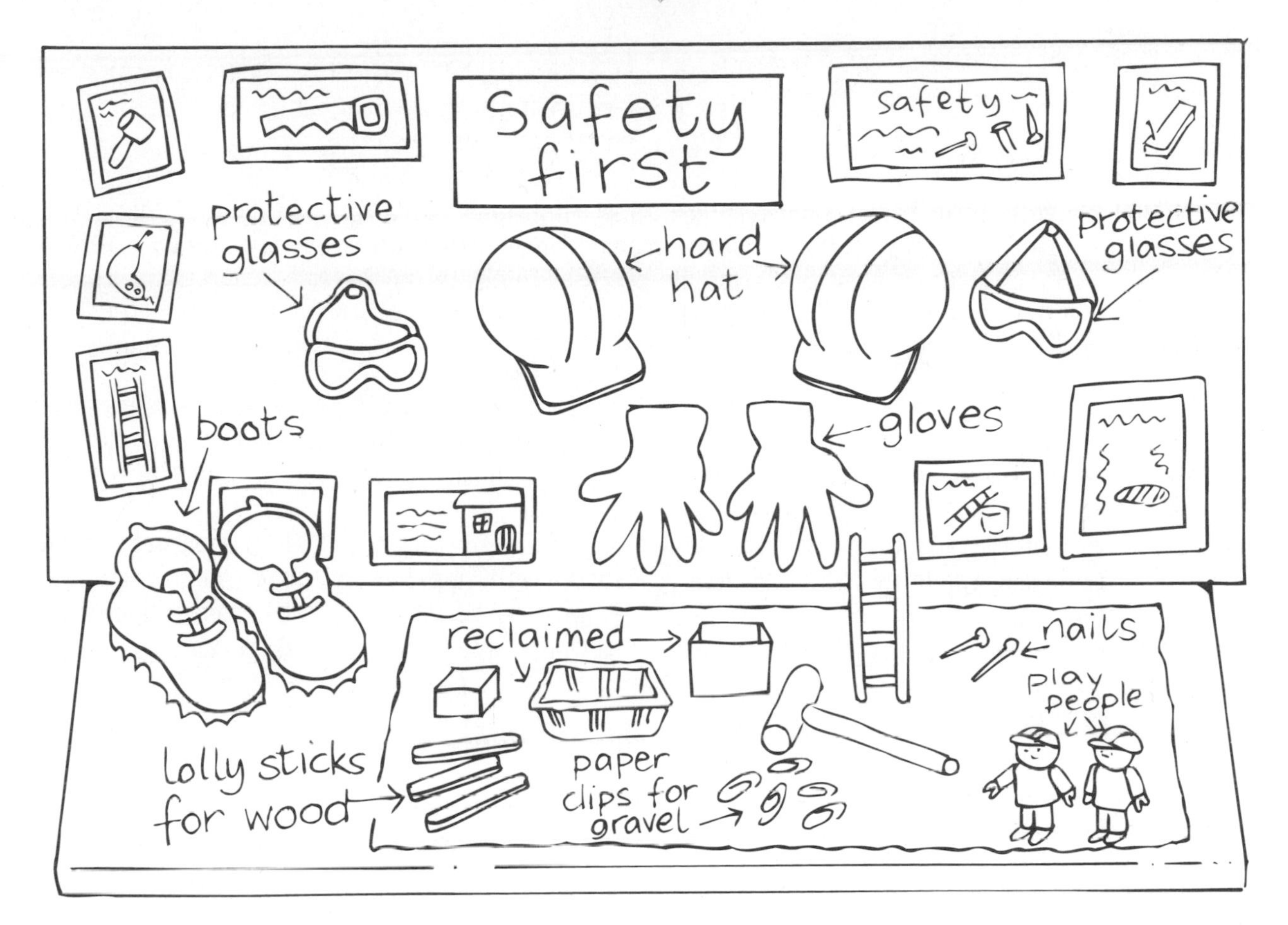

SAFETY FIRST

What you need

Backing paper, table, hard hats, safety glasses, protective face masks, protective gloves and strong boots. Large and small reclaimed boxes including plastic and foil trays, card, silver foil, lolly sticks, used match sticks, paper clips, plastic curls, play people, construction kits including plastic ladders, stapler, nails, hammer and building site safety posters designed in the activity on page 58.

Preparation

Reinforce the importance of safety aspects of the materials found on this display when the children are handling the equipment.

What to do

Staple the backing paper onto the display board and table top. Arrange the children's mounted posters as a border. Remind the children about the items needed to keep safe on the building site. Pick up the safety hat, protective glasses, mask, gloves and boots one at a time, asking the children why they are necessary, which part of the body they protect and why it needs protecting. Attach the items to the display board or place them on the table while the children watch. It may be necessary to staple cardboard shelves and hammer in nails to stand the objects on. Ask the children for suggestions for captions and labels to add to the display board.

Help the children to use the card, reclaimed materials and construction kits to make diggers and cranes for a 'building site' on the table top. Give the children the plastic curls (stones), paper clips (gravel), matchsticks and lolly sticks (wood), silver foil (water hazard), play people and ladders, asking them to complete the scene creating either safe or hazardous scenarios.

Discussion

Why do workers need protecting? What do they need protecting from? What is protective clothing made from? What does dangerous mean? What is dangerous on building sites? Why should care be taken on a building site? Why is protective clothing worn on building sites?

CHAPTER 8 ASSEMBLIES

This chapter provides ideas for assemblies or group sharing times based on the theme of Materials. They will help the children to think about the many materials they use everyday and to realize that we must look after the precious things in our lives.

PRECIOUS THINGS

In this assembly, children can draw on experience they may have had during a range of activities related to the topic. They should have begun to realize that some materials are particularly rare and costly and that others are plentiful and low in price. It will also help to introduce the concept of value: the most precious object is not necessarily the most expensive.

The main focus for this gathering is ***The Tale of Three Trees*** by Angela Elwell Hunt and Tim Jonke (Lion Books). It is an adaptation of a traditional American folk story about three young trees who wish to become a treasure chest, a ship and a pointer to God. Their stories are linked with the birth, life and death of Jesus. The book is beautifully illustrated in full colour.

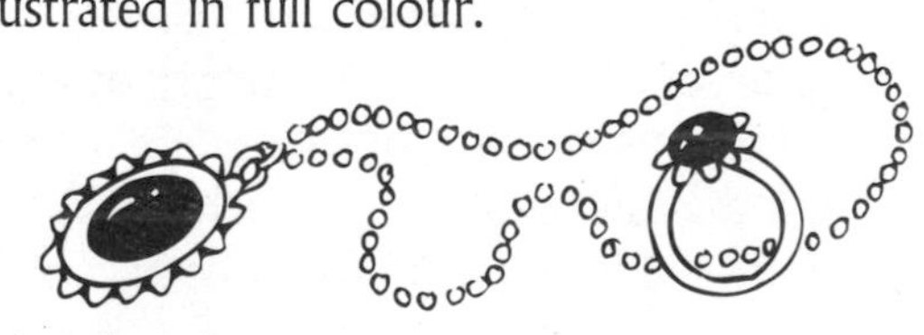

Introduction

As the children enter the assembly area, play a piece of appropriate music such as ***My Favourite Things*** from 'The Sound of Music'.

Show the children a small collection of objects which have each cost a great deal of money – you could include a beautiful piece of jewellery, a complex camera, or a laptop computer. If this is inappropriate, then pictures or posters of expensive items may be used. Emphasize the high price which must be paid for everything you have chosen.

Now display another object which is very precious to you, but which has sentimental rather than financial value – it might be a photograph, a champagne cork, a ticket or a birthday card. Explain why you treasure your chosen item, even though someone else might not understand or appreciate its significance, and emphasize that it is valuable to you because of the memories associated with it.

Activity

Tell the story of ***The Tale of the Three Trees***. In a small group, simply use the text itself, taking care to ensure that all the children are able to see the illustrations easily.

In a larger group, the children could act out the story with appropriate props and costumes. Emphasize the elements of the story which relate to what makes an object truly precious.

Reflection

As the story comes to a close, take a large branch or piece of wood and place it on a table in the centre of the group. If possible, darken the room and shine a single spotlight or anglepoise lamp on the display.

Invite the children to spend a few quiet moments thinking about the story and to reflect on why a simple tree can become very precious indeed.

In silence, ask the children to consider what objects are precious to them and if appropriate, encourage them to share their thoughts with the rest of the group.

Prayer

Some children may wish to listen to a prayer about Jesus who is so important and precious for Christians.

As an alternative, the leader could offer a prayer which lists some of the things which are really valuable in the lives of the children – health, happiness, the love of family and friends.

Music

As the story highlights some of the key events in the life of Jesus, some children might like to listen to or join in with a song which reflects those themes, such as 'Now Jesus one day', in ***Someone's Singing Lord*** (A & C Black).

MAKING A QUILT

This assembly provides an opportunity for children to draw on experiences they may have had during a range of practical activities related to this topic. They should have begun to explore the ways in which different materials may be used together to create something new and beautiful.

The focus for the gathering is *The Patchwork Quilt* by Valerie Flournoy (Picture Puffin). The story tells of a little girl who helps her mother and grandmother to make a quilt using pieces of fabric which represent significant moments in the life of their family. The book has charming illustrations which highlight the closeness between the different generations.

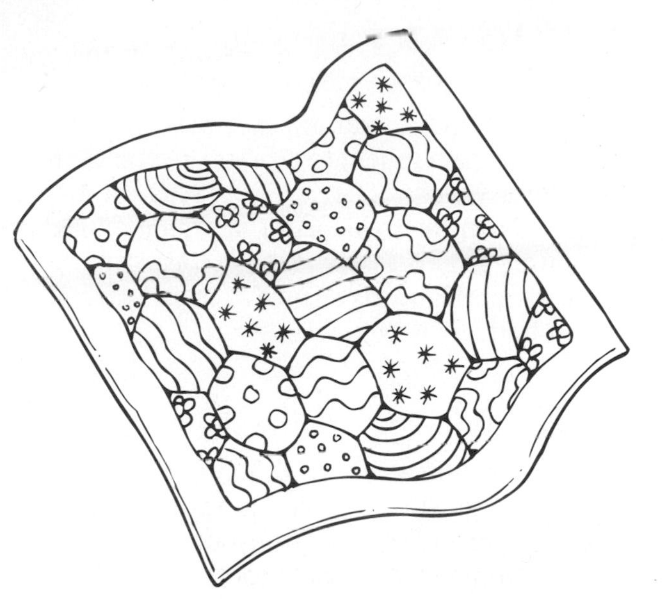

Introduction

Invite the children to sit in a circle and place a large patchwork quilt in the centre of the group. Allow the children to spend a few, quiet moments looking at the quilt in some detail. If it is appropriate, allow them to handle it with care.

Inform the children that the patchwork quilt has been made from many different pieces of fabric in various colours, textures and designs. Give them as much information as possible about the way in which the quilt was constructed.

If the quilt has been made by hand, it may be feasible to invite the individual or group responsible for creating it to come and talk to the children in person about it.

Activity

Read the children the story of *The Patchwork Quilt* or invite them to perform it as a story drama or role play. Emphasize that the materials used in the design are associated with key events in the life of the little girl's family.

Reflection

Invite each child to come forward one by one and place a paper square on a large sheet of card to form their own 'patchwork quilt'. The squares should have been individually decorated in advance of the assembly so that each one is unique and different.

When the 'quilt' is complete, play a piece of quiet, reflective music and encourage the children to consider how one 'quilt' has been made from many parts. Remind them that their assembly is also made up of many individuals who come together to make one whole group.

Prayer

Some children may wish to join in with a short prayer about the importance of difference and diversity within the group which is reflected in the 'quilt' that they have designed and made.

Music

As the children leave the area, play a selection of musical pieces from different cultures and traditions to create a joyful musical patchwork, or sing the song 'Hexagons' on page 83.

CELTIC ART

Throughout the centuries, members of faith communities have sought to express their religious beliefs in a variety of ways. The focus for this assembly is on the Celtic Christian tradition and children are given the opportunity to explore how different materials have been used to create symbolic works of art.

Introduction

As the children enter, play a recording of some contemporary Celtic religious music, such as Liam Lawson's ***Light the Fire*** or works by Iona – these are available through Veritas or St Paul's Multi Media.

Ask the children to sit in a circle around a central display which features a range of different materials – paper, inks, a quill pen, a piece of wood, some metal and a stone or brick.

Encourage the children to spend a few moments looking carefully at the objects and in a small group, allow them to handle some of the items with appropriate care. Invite the children to suggest some of the ways in which they might choose to make use of the materials that form the display.

Activity

Show the children a large map and point out the different Celtic regions – Ireland, Scotland, Wales, Cornwall and Brittany. Tell them that hundreds of years ago, these places were important Christian centres where there were many people who wanted to praise God in as many ways as possible.

Remind the children of the objects which they have seen on the table and inform them of the ways in which the Celts used those materials to share their beliefs about God.

Show the children some pictures, slides or OHP transparencies of illuminated manuscripts such as the Book of Kells or the Lindisfarne Gospels or perhaps some wrapping paper featuring Celtic patterns. Explain that the patterns used have no beginning and no end – just as God has no beginning and no end. Talk about the way in which the manuscripts were produced.

Display other Celtic devotional objects made of wood or metal, such as crosses or statues (use pictures if objects are unavailable). Finally, show some images of Celtic religious buildings and explain that these are also signs of faith.

Reflection

Choose a single object or image as the focus for a few moments of peaceful reflection. Ask the children to sit in silence and study the object or image while listening to some relevant background music. A collection of Gregorian chants might be a good choice or any piece which has a Celtic influence or flavour.

Ask the children to think about some of the reasons why the Celts chose to use their materials in this particular way.

Prayer

This prayer comes from the Celtic tradition and is associated with St Patrick.

Christ be with me, Christ within me,
Christ behind me, Christ before me,
Christ beside me, Christ to win me,
Christ to comfort and restore me,
Christ beneath me, Christ above me,
Christ in quiet, Christ in danger,
Christ in mouth of friend or stranger.

Read the prayer slowly to the children and tell them that even if they do not understand all the words, they may still feel its rhythm and power.

Music

As the children leave the area, play some contemporary Celtic music, such as a piece by the traditional violinist, Martin Hayes.

Collective worship in schools

The assemblies outlined here are suitable for use with children in nurseries and playgroups, but would need to be adapted for use with pupils at registered schools. As a result of legislation enacted in 1944, 1988 and 1993, there are now specific points to be observed when developing a programme of Collective Acts of Worship in a school.

Further guidance will be available from your local SACRE – Standing Advisory Council for RE.

POEMS AND ACTION RHYMES

PATCHY BEAR

I'm a roly-poly
plump teddy bear
with a lopsided smile
and gold coloured fur

I've lost my growl
and a lot of my hair
I'm old and I'm bald
and my fur has gone bare

but I love to be cuddled
and snuggle in bed
I need someone to say
You're my very best Ted

I like listening to stories
to dance and to play
I can keep secrets
and I'll do what you say

I need someone special
a friend just like you
so take care of me
and I'll take care of you.

Joan Poulson

MATERIALS

What's made of metal?
A toaster and a kettle.

What's made of wool?
My scarf and grandma's shawl.

What's made of tin
Our kitchen's pedal-bin

What's made from thread?
The sheets upon my bed.

What's skin and bone?
The body that's my own!

Trevor Harvey

BLOWING GLASS

The ball sparkles
Growing, growing,
The man goes red
Blowing, blowing.
Very soon a shape
Is showing
In the glass
So hot and glowing.

Coral Rumble

PLAYDOUGH PEOPLE

Playdough people
are floppy and fat.
Some wear a funny old
playdough hat,

Playdough people
have playdough faces,
with blobs for noses
and hair like laces.

Playdough people
have bendy legs,
ears like pancakes,
eyes like eggs.

Playdough people
roll up in a ball.
Then playdough people
aren't people at all.

Tony Mitton

PAPER

Paper's very useful
To cut, and stick, and fold,
Paper hankies in a box
For when I've got a cold.

Paper's good to paint on;
Houses, trees and hills,
With a piece of paper towel
For wiping up the spills.

Paper can have stories on,
Made up into books,
Paper with the recipe,
When my Granny cooks.

Paper with some printing on
Telling people news,
Paper on the kitchen floor
For my muddy shoes.

Susan Eames

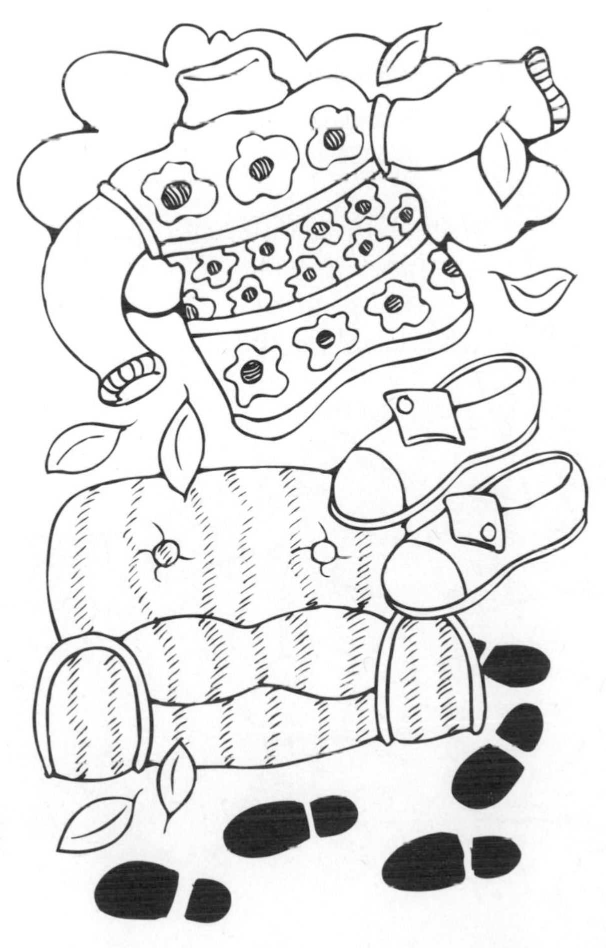

PATTERNS

Pretty flowers all in rows
make a pattern on my clothes.

Stripes of red and blue I see
climbing up our old settee.

Dots and spots just cover all
on the paper on the wall.

Squares and diamonds, circles too
make a pattern on my shoe.

In the garden near the tree
leafy patterns fall on me.

High above clouds blowing by
changing patterns in the sky.

Footprint patterns on the ground
Lots of patterns all around.

Brenda Williams

MISS POLLY

Miss Polly had a dolly
Who was sick, sick, sick
So she 'phoned for the doctor
To be quick, quick, quick
The doctor came
With his bag and his hat,
And he rapped at the door
With a rat-tat-tat.

He looked at the dolly
And he shook his head.
Then he said, 'Miss Polly,
Put her straight to bed.'
He wrote on a paper
For a pill, pill, pill;
'I'll be back in the morning
With my bill, bill, bill.'

Traditional

THE KITCHEN BAND

Take a spoon
and hit a saucepan.
BANG. BANG. BANG.
Can you play
the frying pan?
TWANG. TWANG. TWANG.
Tap some glasses
full of water.
TING. TING. TING.
Beat a rhythm
on a tin,
or better still
a metal bin.

With all these different
things to hand,
you can make a
KITCHEN BAND.

Jan Pollard

BRAND NEW

I like using bits of things
That people throw away.
Like yoghurt pots and coloured strings
And then I like to play.

I mostly like the coloured things
With plastic bits that shine
So I've asked my mum to save those bits
That I can use next time.

I've stuck the things together
With a pot of sticky glue
And I've made a plastic rocket ship
That nearly looks brand new.

She's hung my rocket in my room
So I can fly away.
Tonight I'm flying to the moon
But I'll be back next day.

Stevie Ann Wilde

WHAT ARE THEY LIKE?

Silk is smooth and soft
Like a baby's skin.
Wool is thick and warm.
Cotton's cool and thin.

Paper folds and tears.
Glass lets light in.
Steel is strong and tough
Like a rhino's skin.

John Foster

BUILD A HOUSE WITH BRICKS

Here is the builder
to build a house with bricks.

Here is the carpenter
with wooden doors to fix.

Here's an electrician
putting lights in the hall.

Now comes the plasterer
to plaster on the wall.

Now we have a plumber
fitting pipes to the bath.

Soon we'll have concrete
delivered for a path.

Don't forget the windows
with glass shining bright.

Now our house is finished
and it's strong, warm and light.

Brenda Williams

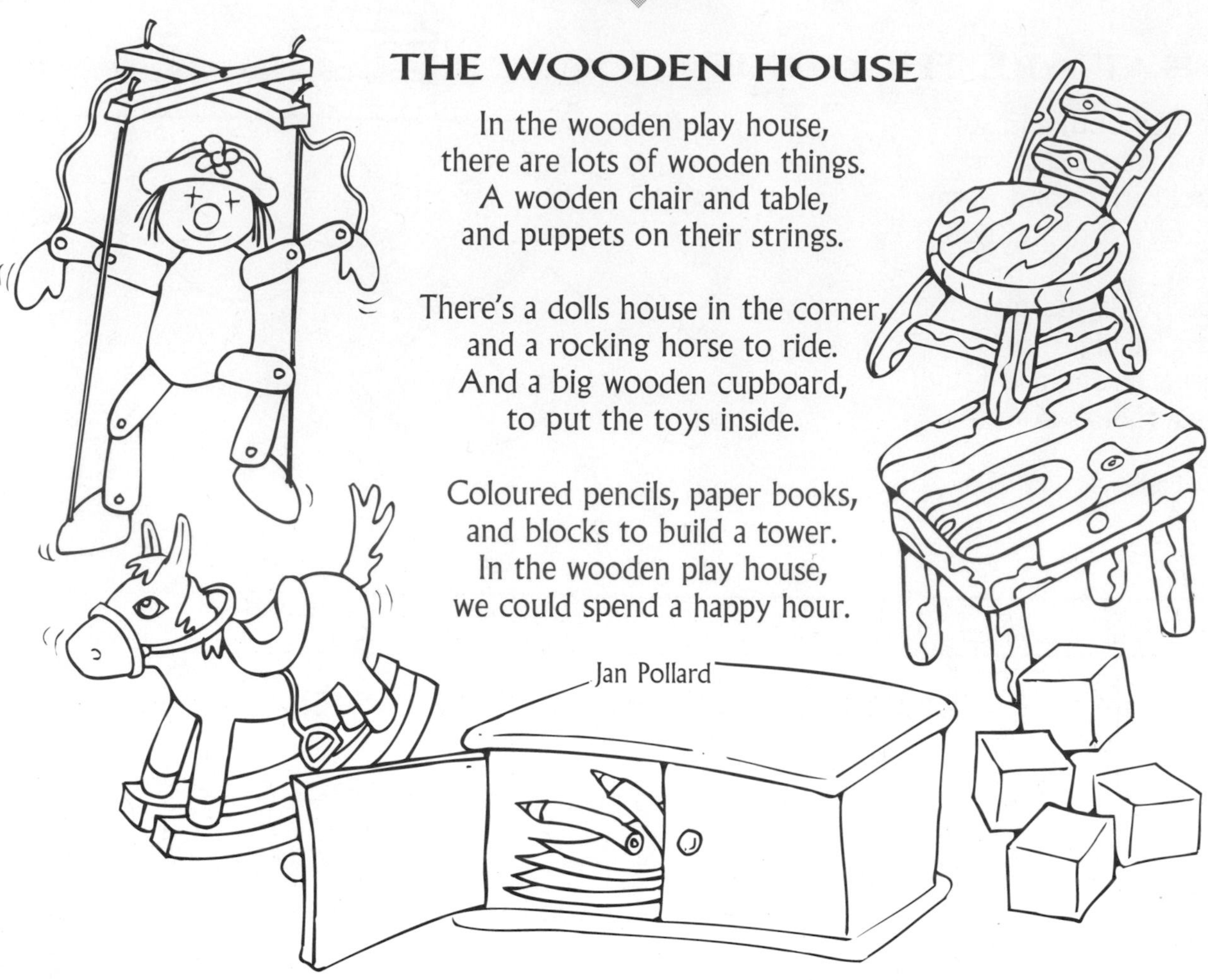

THE WOODEN HOUSE

In the wooden play house,
there are lots of wooden things.
A wooden chair and table,
and puppets on their strings.

There's a dolls house in the corner,
and a rocking horse to ride.
And a big wooden cupboard,
to put the toys inside.

Coloured pencils, paper books,
and blocks to build a tower.
In the wooden play house,
we could spend a happy hour.

Jan Pollard

TREES

When grandpa was a boy of three
He found some acorns by a tree.
He planted them in a row of eight
That followed the path to the garden gate.
For seventy years he watched them grow
Eight oak trees planted in a row.
When I am old, as old as he
I wonder how many trees we'll see.
For every day a tree is cut
To make a table, door or hut.
Paper too comes from a tree,
Pencils, books and boats at sea
So I must plant trees if I can
To see some left when I'm a man.

Brenda Williams

SWINGING

My grandma has a garden gate
I like to swing upon.
The metal sides are very straight
The gate is very strong.
She says it's called wrought iron work
With leaves and twirls and things.
It may be her best garden gate
But to me it's just a swing!

Stevie Ann Wilde

MOVE LIKE A ROBOT

I'm a metal robot,
made of tin.
And this is the box,
that I came in.
Put in a battery.
Off I go.
Not too fast,
and not too slow.

Up goes one arm.
ONE – TWO – THREE
Up goes the other arm,
as jerky as can be.
I turn my head,
to see what I can see.
And jerk my legs.
ONE – TWO – THREE

Walk like a robot.
ONE – TWO – THREE
I'm a metal robot.
Move like me.

Jan Pollard

THERE'S A HOLE IN MY PANTS

There's a hole in my pants.
It's our washing machine.
It's eating our clothes,
Not washing them clean.

As it churns round and round,
It snorts and it snickers,
Chewing holes in Dad's shirts
And ripping Mum's knickers.

It's swallowed a sock.
We can't open the door.
It's bubbling out soap suds
All over the floor.

There's a monster that lives
In our washing machine.
It's eating our clothes,
Not washing them clean.

John Foster

STORIES

LITTLE WOODEN TRAIN

Uncle Sam brought Lucy a present.

It was a little wooden train.

It just fitted into Lucy's hand, poking out a little bit each end when she curled her fingers around it.

The train had an engine and two carriages. The engine was red and the carriages were blue. Each one had six yellow wheels. The engine had six red wheels.

'It's a very special train,' Uncle Sam said. 'An old man made it. He cut it all out of a good piece of wood – even the wheels – and he smoothed it all down and painted it. It was very hard work for him.'

Dad said, 'In that case, Lucy, you'd better take extra special care of it!'

At first, Lucy did try to take very good care of the little wooden train. She put it on the cupboard by the side of her bed and just looked at it.

But she liked the feel of it so much that she wanted to hold it in her hand. It felt very smooth. She could run her fingers along it and they never caught anywhere. It felt like a nice shape, too.

Lucy got to be so fond of her little wooden train that she had to take it out to play. She carried it very carefully into the garden, and placed it on a brick. She put some more bricks alongside the first one, to make a railway track. She ran the train along the brick track.

Some of the red and yellow paint came off the wheels. Somehow they didn't look quite so good. In fact, they looked a little bit scratched.

Lucy hid the little wooden train into one of her drawers, and crossed her fingers that nobody would see it.

She left the train in the drawer for a few days. But on Thursday, Mrs Jones said, 'Has anybody got anything favourite they could bring to show the class tomorrow?' and Lucy knew that she just had to take the train into school.

After all, it was her very favourite thing of all.

She got some kitchen roll and wrapped the train very carefully in it. Then she poked it into one of the pockets of her schoolbag, before Dad could see it. What would he say if he knew she'd spoiled it?

After all, Uncle Sam had said the train was very, very special, and Dad had said that she would have to take extra special care of it.

At school everybody wanted to have a go with Lucy's train. Melanie borrowed it first and when the teacher called them for drinks she accidentally dropped it in the water tray and left it there in her hurry.

When they looked for it afterwards, all the water had soaked into it, and its shine was gone. They tried to dry it on the paper towels, but the shine wouldn't come back.

Sandeep borrowed the little wooden train next, and he took it outside to where the children had built a little town with railway lines and car parks in the dirt. The train got a little bit buried and somebody casually stood on it and it got buried a bit more and scratched by a stone... and when Lucy got it back it looked in a very sad state indeed.

It went on all day, with everyone having a go with Lucy's little wooden train, and the poor little train getting more and more battered.

By the time she went home Lucy's little wooden train looked worn and tired-out, but it still fitted nice and snug in her hand. Lucy put her hand, with the train in it, in her pocket, and thought she would just try to keep it safe. 'Thank you for bringing your little wooden train, Lucy,' Mrs Jones said. 'I think all the children liked it better than anything else!'

Lucy was pleased about that.

But she wasn't so pleased when Dad came home from work. 'Got a surprise for you, Lucy!' he said. 'Uncle Sam's coming tonight.'

Oh no! What on earth was she going to do?

Up in her bedroom, Lucy took the little wooden train out of her pocket and looked at it.

It was a very sorry sight indeed. And Uncle Sam was bound to ask about it! Whatever was she to do?

She tried rubbing it and polishing it and trying to knock the bumps out on the cupboard, but nothing helped. In fact, they only made the little wooden train worse.

And then there was a ring at the doorbell. 'Lucy!' Dad called up the stairs. 'Here's Uncle Sam. Come and say hello!'

Lucy decided the best thing to do would be to admit her problem right away. She said, 'I'm really sorry, Uncle Sam. I really am. I know the wooden train is special but everybody loves it and...'

Uncle Sam listened patiently, his head on one side. 'Let's have a look at it then,' he said.

Slowly, Lucy pulled the little wooden train from her pocket. Uncle Sam took it from her and held it up to the light and turned it this way and that... and then he began to laugh.

Lucy could hardly believe her ears. She had ruined the train and now Uncle Sam was laughing. Why?

'Well,' said Uncle Sam, his eyes twinkling. 'I reckon this has got to be the best-used toy in the whole wide world, Lucy! If you had never played with it at all it would be as good as new, wouldn't it? And that would mean you'd just left it in the cupboard and looked at it. But I can see – because it's so worn you must have played with it all the time. You must love it very much indeed!'

And she did, didn't she?

Irene Yates

THE NEWSPAPER PRINCESS

'Mum! Mum! shouted Ellie as she and her friend, Ben ran to the school gate to meet Mrs Archer. 'We're going to have a Summer Fête in July... and there's a fancy dress competition!'

'That's nice,' said Mrs Archer. She put Ellie's lunchbox into her shopping bag and they set off for home. 'What do you want to be?'

'Oh, I don't know yet,' said Ellie. 'Jasmin says she's going to be a princess, with a crown and a long silky dress.'

'Billy Bates wants to be Father Christmas!' said Ben.

'Father Christmas? In July?' laughed Ellie's mum.

'I think he just wants a sackful of presents!' said Ellie. 'And he'll keep them all for himself.'

'Wish I'd thought of that,' said Ben, grinning.

'I'd like to be something... special,' said Ellie.

'I don't mind what I am, as long as it's Batman,' said Ben, and he did a quick turn around a lamp-post, pretending to fly.

They reached Ben's house and he left them with a wave.

'Well,' said Ellie's mum as they walked on. 'Whatever you are, it'll have to be cheap and cheerful. I'm afraid I can't afford to buy anything, you know.'

Ellie didn't say anything. She would have loved to be a princess like Jasmin, in a beautiful dress, but she knew it was out of the question.

'Don't worry, Ellie,' said her mum, squeezing her hand. 'I've already got an idea.'

As the days passed and the Summer Fête drew nearer, Jasmin showed off more and more about the wonderful dress that had been specially made for her to wear to the fête. 'It's bound to win first prize!' she told the class.

But still Mrs Archer hadn't done anything about Ellie's costume.

Ellie didn't like to pester her. She asked Ben if he knew anything. Ben's mum was Mrs Archer's best friend. 'Haven't a clue, Ellie,' he said. 'But she has been collecting a lot of junk from mum lately.'

'Junk?'

'Yeah – you know, for recycling and stuff. Mum said she's going to make something with it.'

Ellie was horrified. Junk! Everyone would laugh at her – especially Jasmin. That evening, while her mum was watching television, Ellie sneaked a look in the cupboard under the stairs. It was full of boxes, tin foil, paper, bubble wrap and other strange things that they normally took to the recycle dump. Ellie closed the door quietly and went back into the living room.

'Mum,' she said, 'you don't have to worry about fancy dress after all. I can go in ordinary clothes. I expect it'll be too hot to dress up, anyway.'

'That's all right, Ellie,' said her mum. 'I've got it all worked out. You'll see!'

Ellie's heart sank. She would just have to hope she didn't look too terrible.

The sun shone through Ellie's window and woke her. It was Saturday, the day of the Summer Fête. Ellie felt sick. She knew it was going to be awful.

Downstairs, her worst fears came true when she found her mum in the kitchen surrounded by the bags of rubbish. The table was covered with a mess of sticky tape, string, scissors and face paints.

'Here you are, Ellie,' said her mum. 'I just want to put your costume together. It won't take long.'

Ellie watched silently while her mum folded newspapers, cut up plastic bags and bubble wrap, snipped, taped, pinned and tied. She tried hard to eat some breakfast, but it wouldn't go down somehow. She couldn't believe what was happening. At last, when all was in place, her mum made up Ellie's face with face paints.

'Here. The finishing touch,' said her mum. 'I made this one earlier.' She put a crown on Ellie's head made from the bottom of a plastic lemonade bottle. Ellie ran to look at herself in the hall mirror. 'Wow!' she gasped.

She wore an amazing, flouncy skirt made from pleated newspapers, bubble wrap and left-over pea netting. The top of her dress was a large paper bag, with holes cut out for her head and arms. A large, yellow, smiley sun was stuck on the front, cut out of yellow fabric, and the words: SMILE – I'M SAVING THE PLANET were painted across it. Down her back hung a cloak made from transparent plastic, cut into strips, and oddments of ribbon. And everywhere, her mum had stuck on shiny stars and paper flowers – even the tops of her sandals. Ellie had large, pink spots on her cheeks, black spikey eyelashes and a wide smiley mouth.

'I'm a Newspaper Princess!' she laughed, and ran to hug her mum.

They collected Ben on the way to the fête. He roared out of his house wearing black leggings, bright blue swimming shorts and a black T-shirt, while he held out a black plastic coat which flared out behind him. 'Da-da da-da da-da da-da... Batman!' he sang out. 'Gosh, Ellie,' he said, when he saw her. 'You look brilliant! Bet you win!'

Ellie's costume did indeed win first prize, and Ellie was amazed. But the judges said it showed how things we usually throw away can be used for good ideas. It set a very good example to everybody. Even Ben won a prize for being such a keen Batman, charging round in front of the judges with tireless energy.

As for Jasmin, her dress and sparkly crown were very pretty but she didn't win a prize and she threw such a tantrum, that her parents had to take her home early.

Jackie Andrews

POLLY AND THE PATCHWORK QUILT

Polly loved going to her Gran's house. Gran could always think of lots of exciting things to do. Sometimes they baked cakes, or painted pictures, or strung coloured beads on thread.

One day Polly found Gran kneeling in front of a big cardboard box.

'Oh, I'm glad you're here, Polly,' said Gran. 'You can help me pick out some fabrics.

'What are fabrics, Gran?' asked Polly.

'Look in the box and you'll see,' Gran replied.

Polly looked in the box. Inside were all sorts of different pieces of cloth all jumbled up together. They were every colour of the rainbow.

'What do you want them for, Gran?' asked Polly.

'I'm going to make a patchwork quilt for the baby coming. For your new little brother or sister.'

Polly was very excited about the new baby who was growing in Mummy's tummy. It was going to be born in the spring.

'Pick out the prettiest pieces of fabric you can find,' said Gran, 'then I'll sew them all together to make the quilt.'

Polly pulled out a piece of bright red cloth. It felt soft under her fingers.

'What's this, Gran?' she asked.

'That's velvet,' said Gran. 'It's a piece of your old party frock. When you grew out of it, I asked Mummy to give me some for my fabric box.'

'But how can it be velvet if it's called fabric?' asked Polly.

'Each different kind of fabric has a different name' replied Gran.

Polly pulled out a piece of yellow striped cloth.

'What's this, Gran?' she asked.

'It's cotton,' said Gran. 'That was a lovely summer dress your Mummy had when she was just a little girl like you.'

'I know cotton,' Polly said, 'It's what my white socks are made of.'

Gran smiled.

'You're a clever girl. That's quite right.'

Gran pulled out a piece of brown cloth and handed it to Polly.

'What do you think this fabric is, Polly?' she asked.

Polly felt it. It was brown and rather scratchy. It wasn't soft like the velvet. The feel of it reminded her of something. It was just like a skirt her Mummy wore sometimes. Now what was it called? Polly thought hard.

'Give me a clue,' she said.

'Well, it rhymes with weed,' said Gran.

'I know, I know!' cried Polly, 'It's called tweed!'

'Quite right. Full marks to you,' said Gran and she gave Polly a kiss.

'But we shan't use tweed for the quilt, shall we, Polly? It would feel far too scratchy on baby's soft skin.'

Polly bounced in her chair with excitement at the thought of the new baby. For the first time she noticed the fabric of the chair she was bouncing in.

'What's this, Gran?' she asked feeling the cloth under her. There were big flowers all over it.

Oh, that has a funny name,' said Gran. 'It's called chintz'.

'Chintz,' repeated Polly. She liked the sound of the word.

'What are my dungarees made of, Gran?'

'Denim. They're made of blue denim,' answered Gran.

Polly looked at her Gran's flowery dress and the scarf around her neck.
Then she looked at the curtains and the carpet and all around the room.

'So lots of things are made of fabric, then?'

'Yes, lots of things,' said Gran. 'Now go on, pick me out some more pieces from the box. You're my little helper and you and I are going to make this quilt together.'

Polly was pleased to be called Gran's little helper. She looked carefully through all the pieces of fabric in the box. There were so many and they were all quite different. Not just different colours, but different patterns too. She picked out the prettiest pieces she could find. For each bit she chose, Gran told her the story of what it had once been. Polly loved Gran's stories, especially the ones about long ago.

The last piece Polly chose was a square of shiny pink fabric. It felt soft and slippery and was very beautiful.

'What's this, Gran?' she asked.

'That's called satin,' said Gran. Then she said, 'It's a piece of my wedding dress, Polly. Part of the frock I wore when I married your Grandad.'

'Oh,' said Polly, 'I think this piece should go right in the middle of the baby's quilt then.'

Time passed and spring arrived. The day came when Polly and her Gran tiptoed in to see the new baby, who was lying in a little cot beside Mummy's bed. The baby was very sweet and small and had a tuft of soft black hair. Polly touched it gently.

'That's not fabric, is it, Gran?' she whispered.

'No, dear,' said Gran, laughing, 'that's the baby's hair.'

Then Gran unwrapped the patchwork quilt made of all the different fabrics Polly had chosen. Mummy was very pleased with it. Gran handed it to Polly and carefully, very carefully, Polly laid it over her baby brother and tucked him in, all cosy and warm.

Claire Nielson

1, 2, 3, 4 EV'RYBODY PLAY

In this song small groups play on the verses while everybody plays and/or claps on the chorus. Add further verses according to the instruments available and the experience of your children. Ask them what 'sound' words they would use for each instrument and adapt the verses as necessary:

Verses
Click, click, click go the rhythm sticks...
Ting, ting, ting go the triangles...
Rum te tum go all the drums...

Jean Gilbert

BUILDING

Begin by clapping the percussion rhythm
then let the children use percussion instruments
such as woodblocks or tambourines.

2. Build the chimney, build the roof,
(Tap tap tap, tap tap tap)
Tiles to make it waterproof,
(Tap tap tap, tap tap tap)
While you're building sing this song
(Tap tap tap, tap tap tap)
Make our building nice and strong.
(Tap tap tap, tap tap tap)

Johanne Levy

FAVOURITE FABRICS

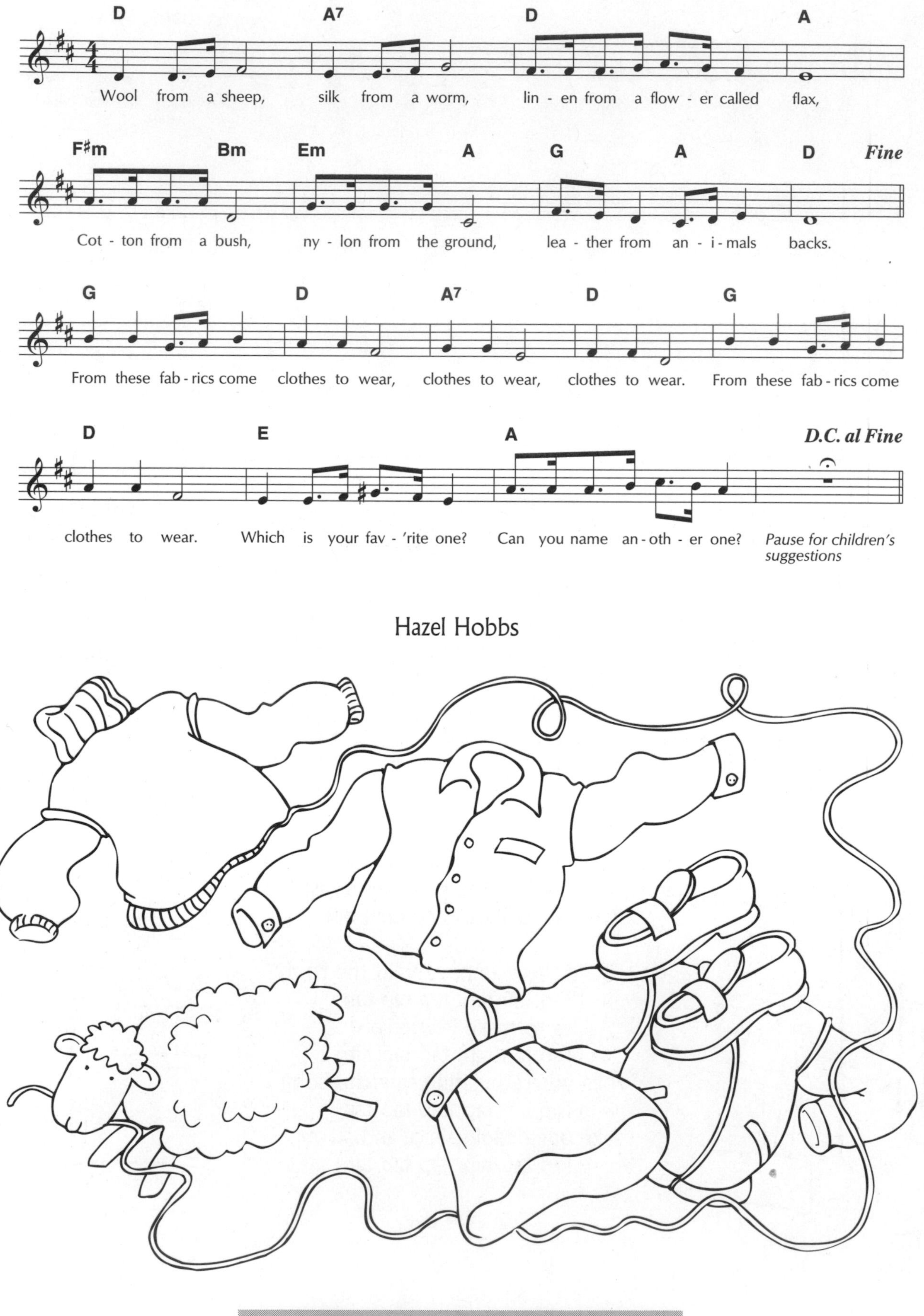

Hazel Hobbs

HEXAGONS
(PATCHWORK CALYPSO)

PAPER COMES FROM TREES

PLASTIC

Let three or four children take turns to name items made from plastic each time you sing the song. Keep going until you run out of ideas!

Hazel Hobbs

RUB A DUB DUB

Words – Pat Sweet
Tune – traditional

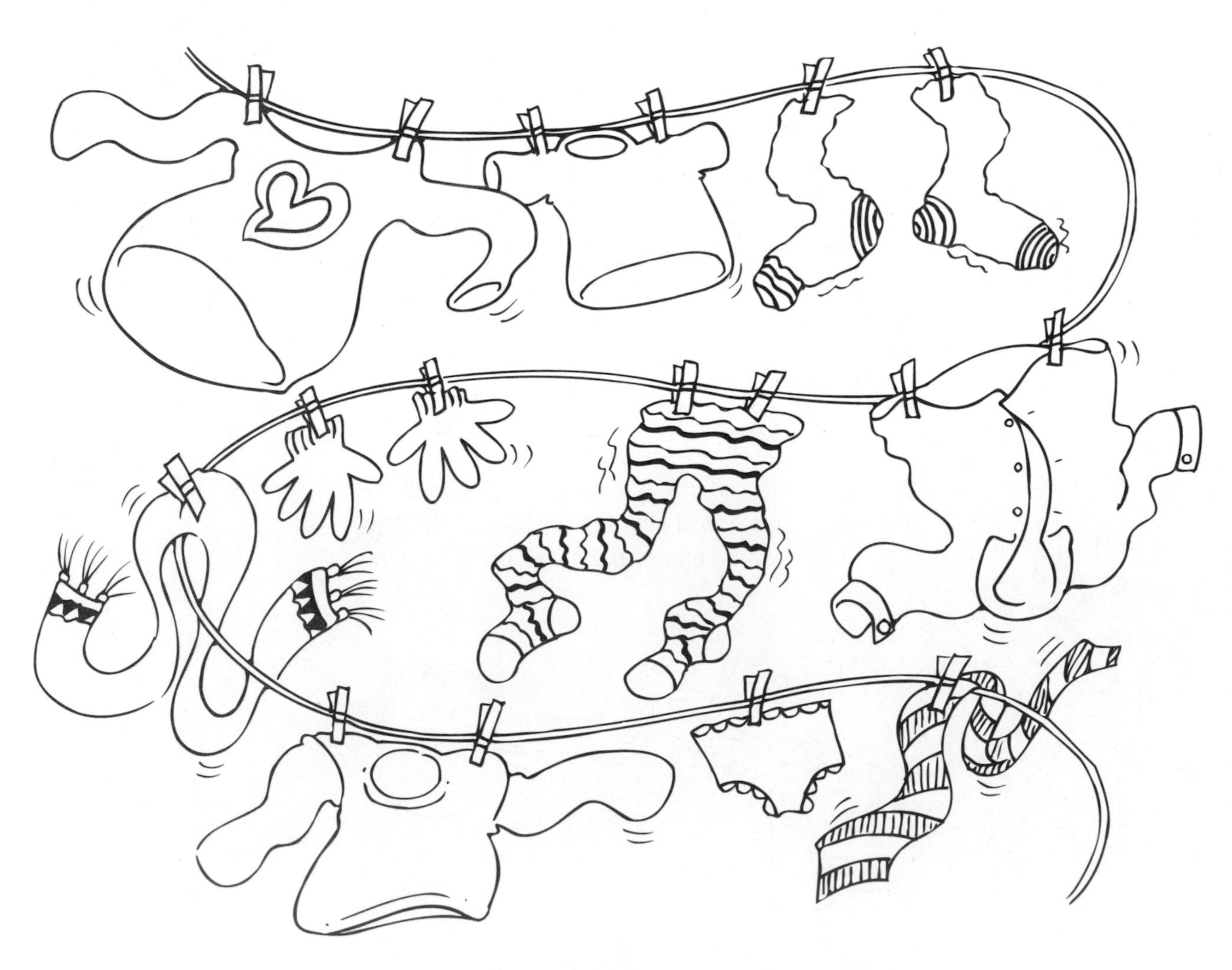

TAP, TAP, TAP

2. Tap (tap, tap) with a wooden spoon...
3. Tap (tap, tap) with a metal spoon...
4. Tap (tap, tap) now with all the spoons...

Give each child a different type of spoon.
Sing the song four times.
When the children hear the correct verse for their type of spoon, encourage them to tap the beat on their hand with the spoon.
Let them do this all the way through the song or just on the 'tap, tap' parts.

Susan Eames

THE BIG BAD WOLF

2. Three little pigs, three little pigs,
The second little pig built a house of twigs,
What would you do? What would you do
If the big bad wolf came chasing after pigs?

3. Three little pigs, three little pigs,
The third little pig built a house of bricks,
What would you do? What would you do
If the big bad wolf kept getting up to tricks?

Susan Eames

Name ____________________

How is it made?

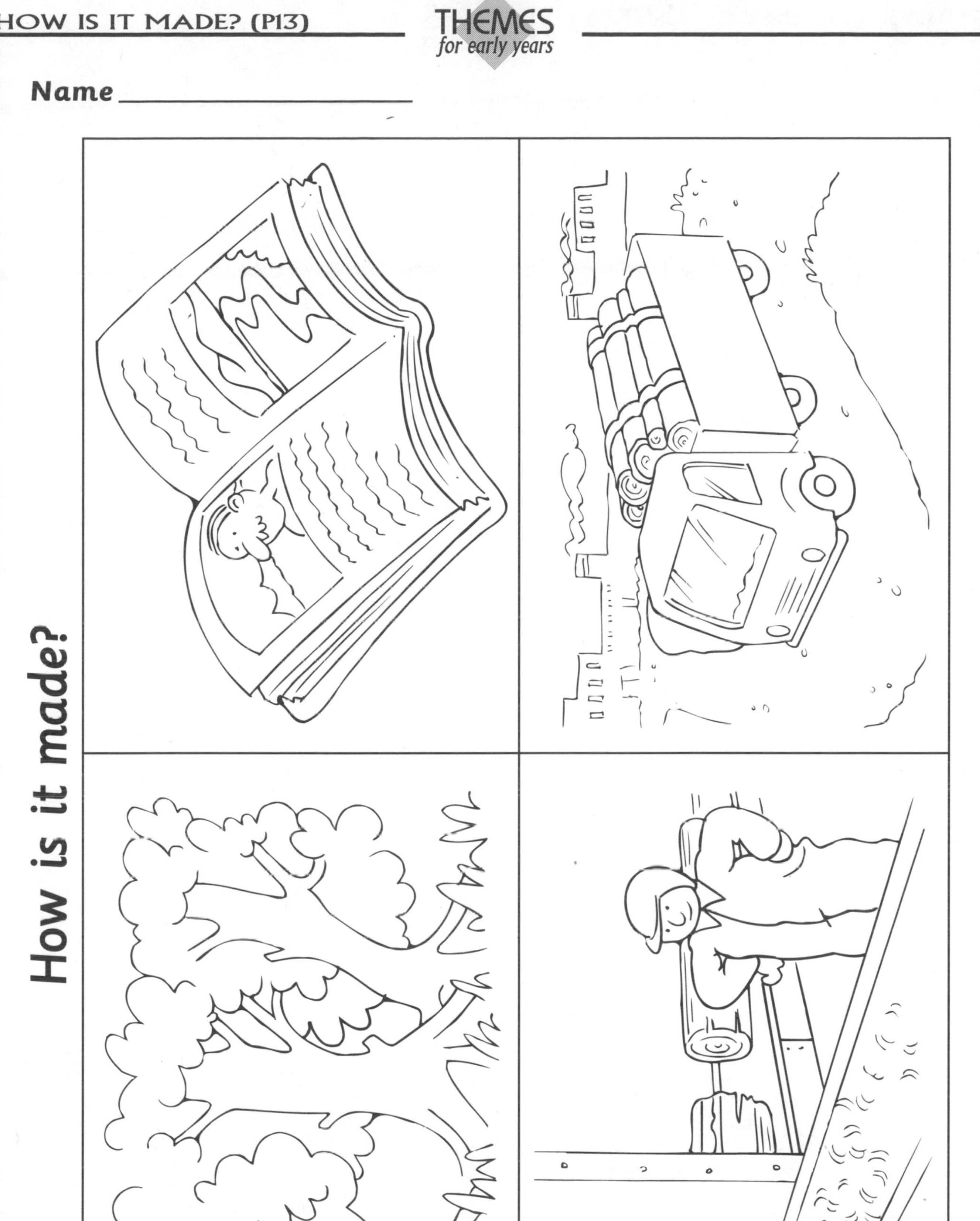

THEMES
for early years

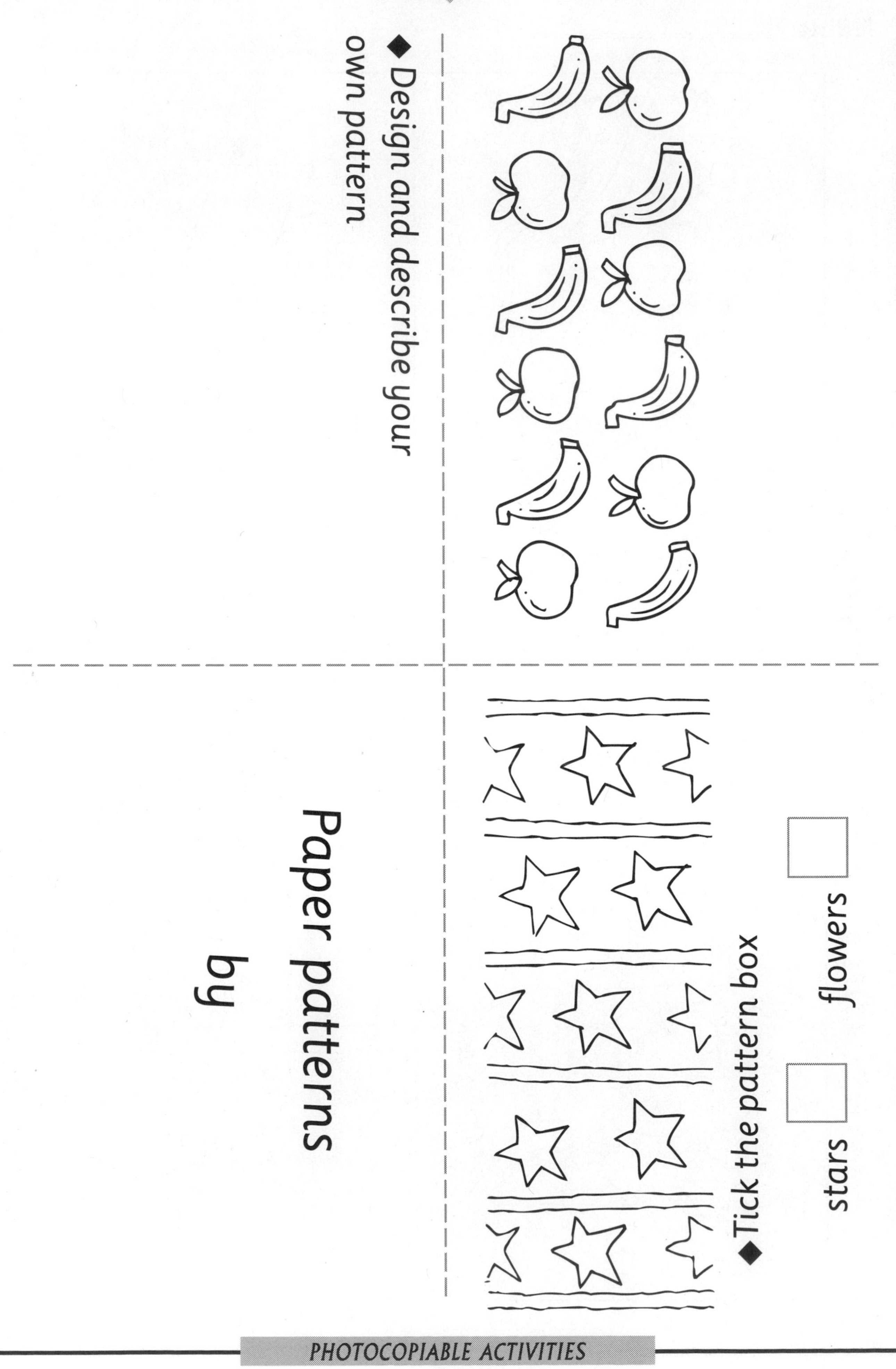
Design and describe your own pattern
Paper patterns
by
Tick the pattern box
stars
flowers

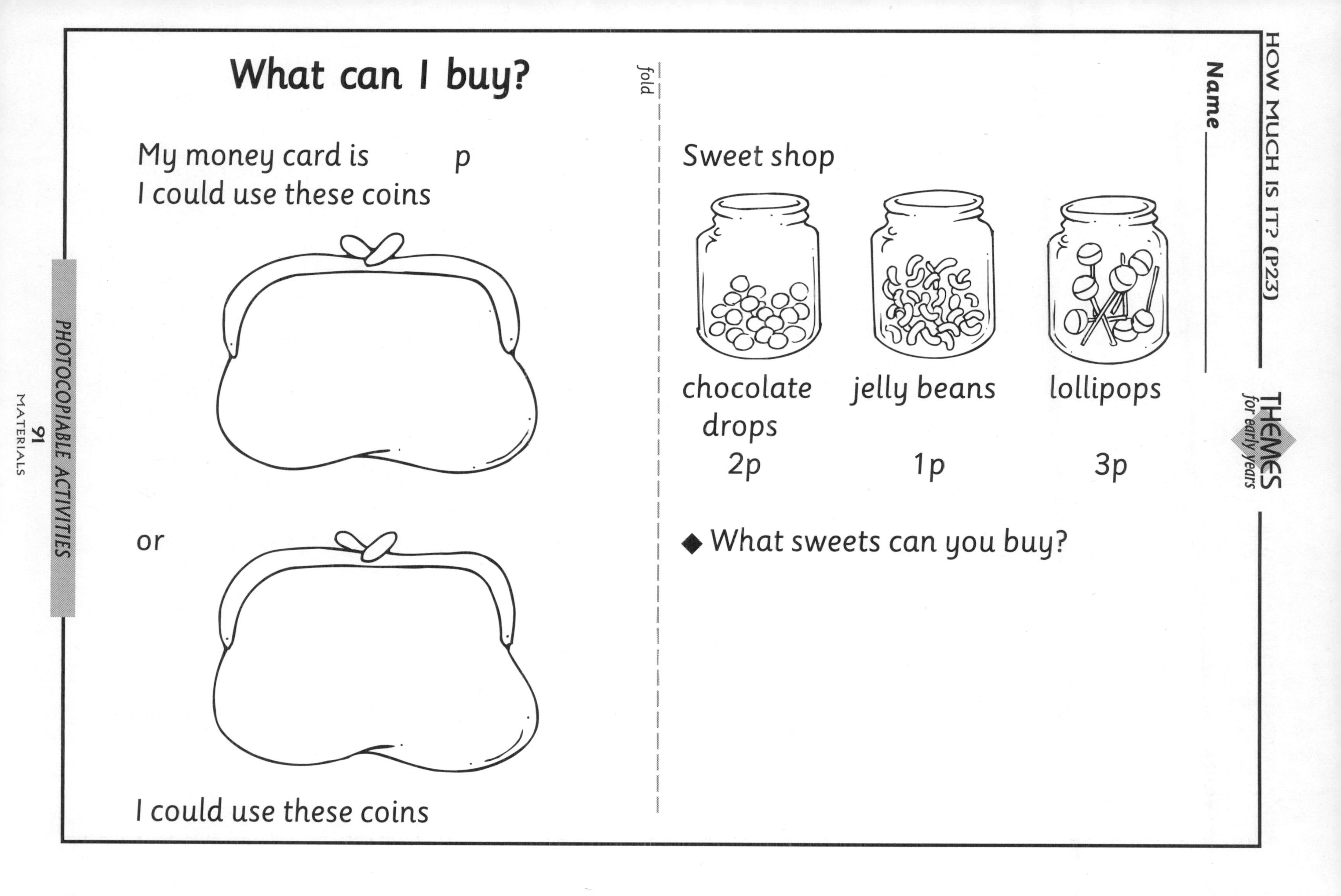

Name ______________________

What can I buy?

My money card is p

I could use these coins

or

I could use these coins

fold

Sweet shop

chocolate drops 2p

jelly beans 1p

lollipops 3p

◆ What sweets can you buy?

Name ____________________

Hexa-friend

◆ Draw yourself in the middle hexagon and all your friends around you.

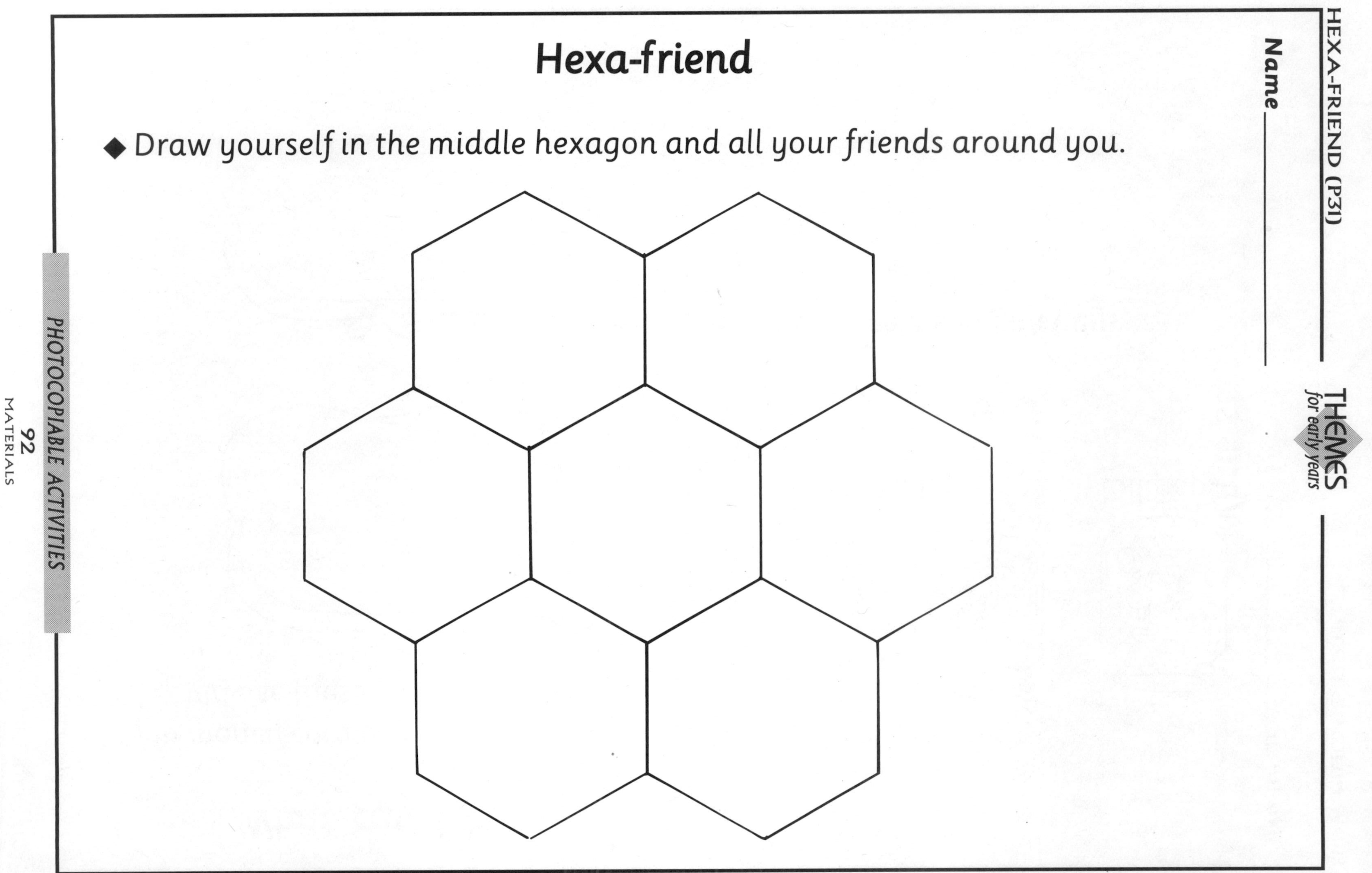

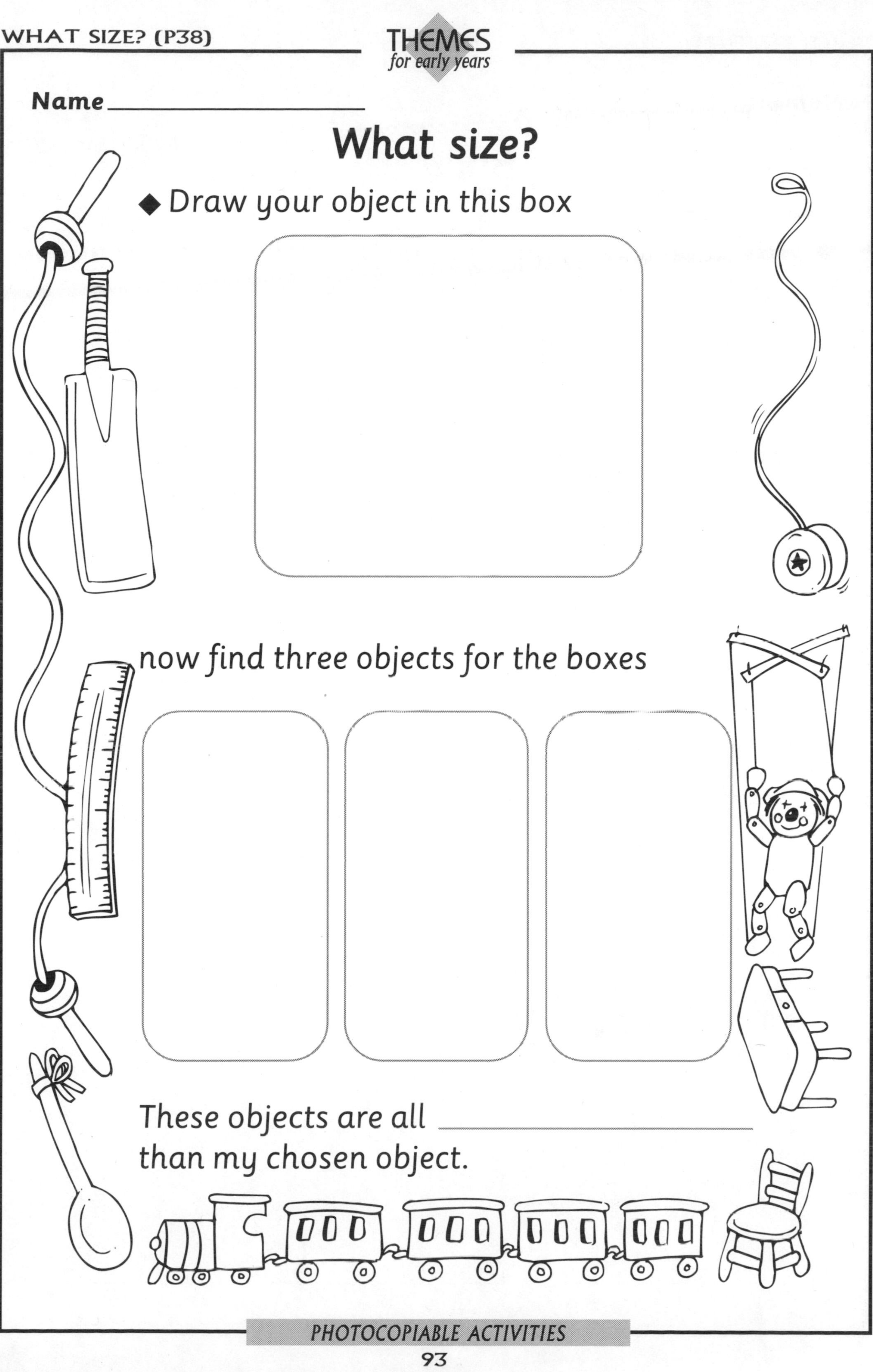

Name ____________________

What size?

◆ Draw your object in this box

now find three objects for the boxes

These objects are all ____________________
than my chosen object.

Name ____________________

Build it!

◆ Draw a picture of your fire-engine helping to rescue the cat.

◆ Draw the parts you used in this box.

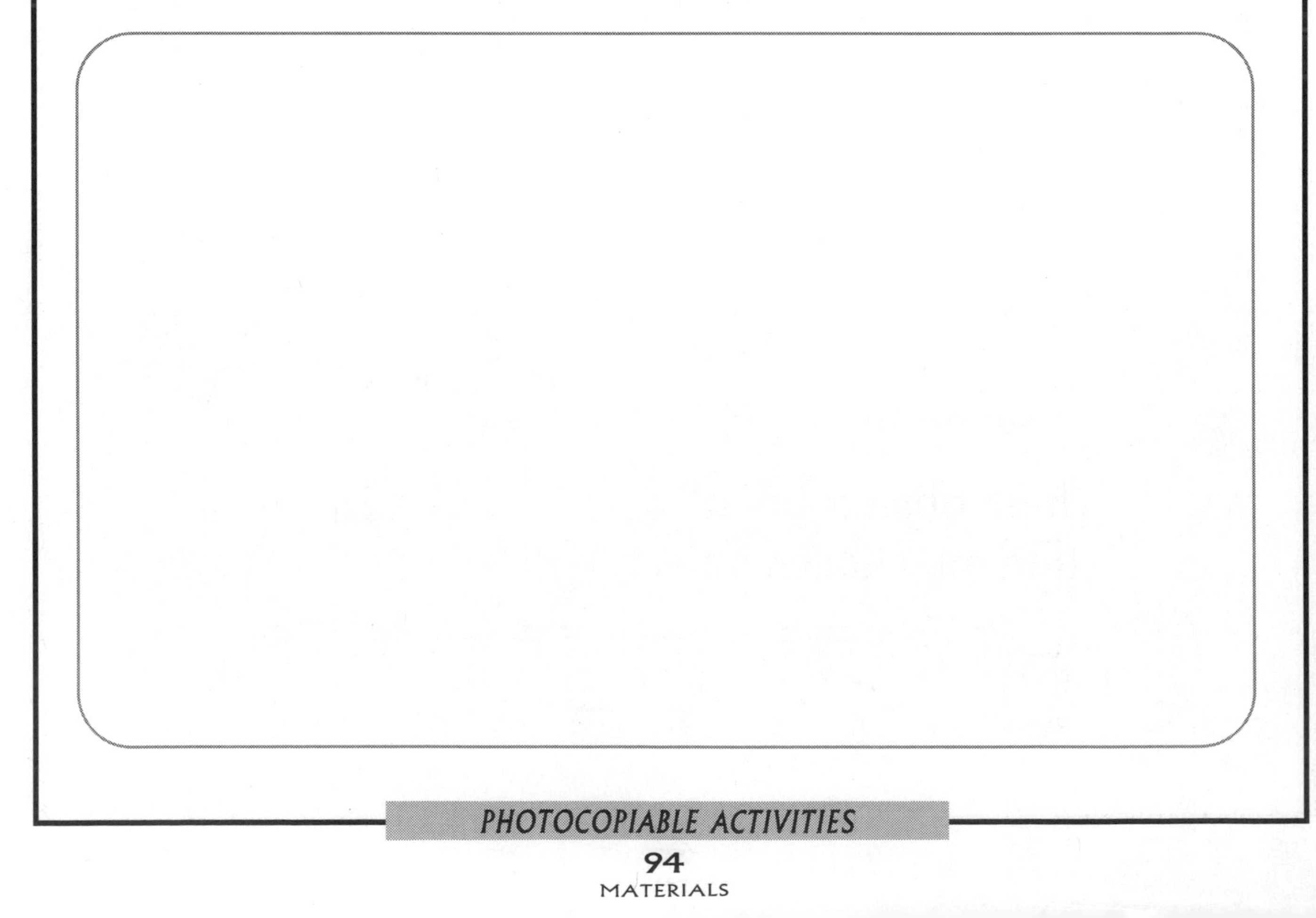

Name ____________

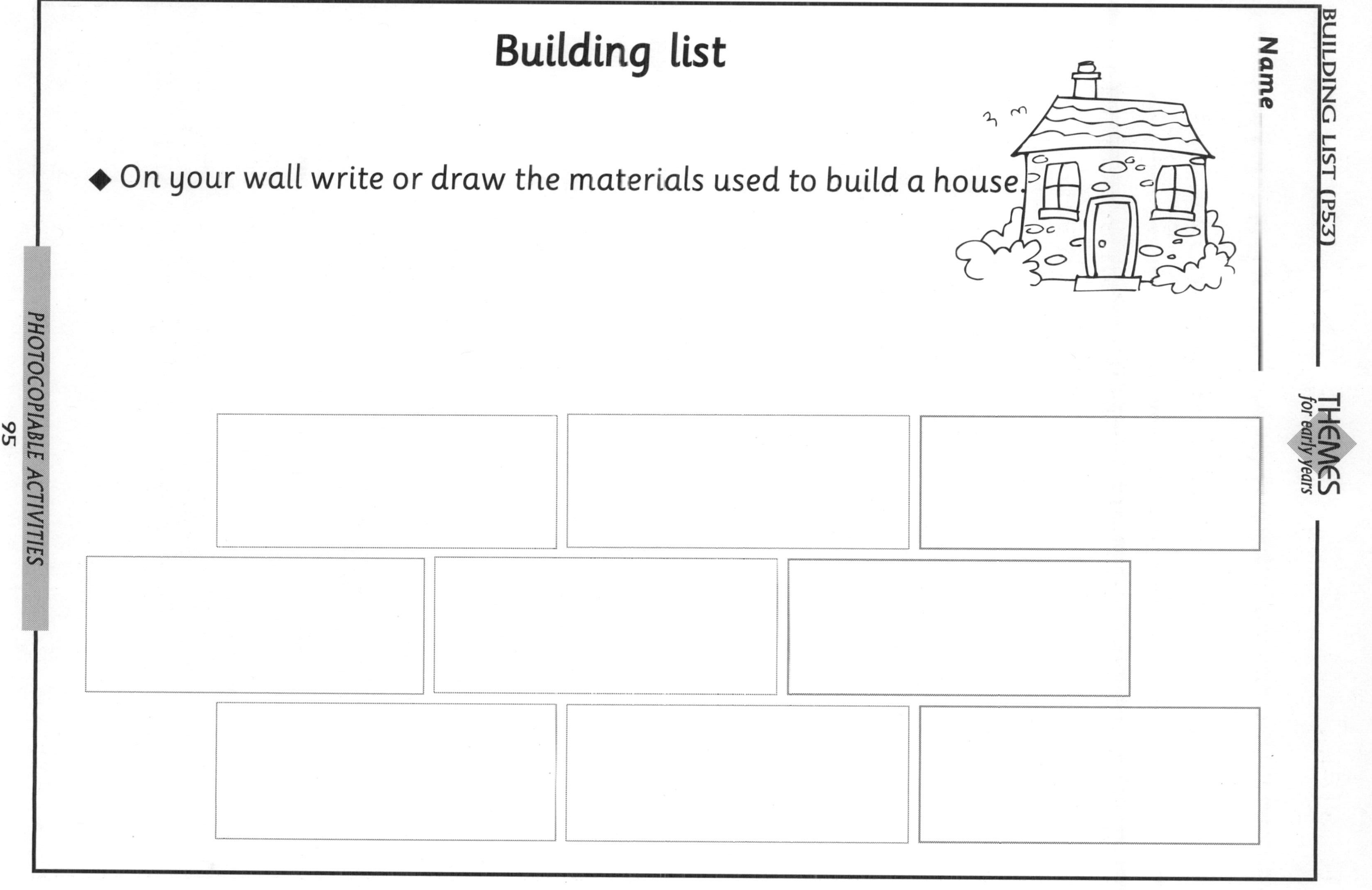

Building list

◆ On your wall write or draw the materials used to build a house.

RECOMMENDED MATERIALS

MUSIC AND SONGS

'The Three Little Pigs', 'The Shoemaker and the Elves', 'The Hairy Scarey Castle', 'Noah's Ark' and 'Goldilocks and the Three Bears' from ***Three Singing Pigs*** (A & C Black)
'I'm walking like a robot' and 'Don't drop litter!' from ***Bobby Shaftoe, clap your hands*** (A & C Black)
'Garage Round', 'My Favourite Things', 'Matchstalk Men and Matchstalk Cats and Dogs' and 'Paddy McGinty's Goat' from ***Hullabaloo-Balay*** (Macmillan Education Ltd)
'Sucking cider through a straw', 'I'm forever blowing bubbles' and 'My grandfather's clock' from ***Ta-ra-ra boom-de-ay*** (A & C Black)
'Hole in the ground', 'Drill, ye tarriers, drill', 'This old hammer' and 'Where did you get that hat?' from ***The Jolly Herring*** (A & C Black)
'Don't you think we're lucky?', 'There's room enough for you' and 'If I had a hammer' from ***Every Colour Under the Sun*** (Ward Lock Educational)
'Chinatown dragon', 'The umbrella man' and 'Pull the cracker-BANG!' from ***Harlequin*** (A & C Black)
'Just a load of rubbish' and 'Chinese New Year' from ***High Low Dolly Pepper*** (A & C Black)
'Tarry wool', 'The tidy song', 'Don't bother me', 'The swing', 'The green dress', 'Uncle Joe, Scarecrow' and 'I have a little tiny house' from ***The Music Box Songbook*** (BBC Enterprises Ltd)
'The wise man and the foolish man' from ***Okki-tokki-unga*** (A & C Black)

POETRY

'Mrs Magee' by Dennis Lee, 'Granny Goat' by Brian Moses, 'The Mud-pie Makers Rhyme' by Janet Paisley, 'Mud' by Ann Bonner, 'Plasticine' by Wendy Cope, from ***Twinkle Twinkle Chocolate Bar*** (Oxford University Press)
'Play shop' by Celia Warren, 'Whoops!' by Judith Nicholls from ***An Orange Poetry Paintbox*** (Oxford University Press)
'The Cave' by Tony Mitton, 'Our dragon' by Wendy Larmont from ***A Purple Poetry Paintbox*** (Oxford University Press)
'My Den' by Tony Mitton, 'Castle' by Tony Mitton, 'High and Dry' by Tony Mitton, 'We've got to start recycling' by John Foster and 'Grandad Says' by Irene Yates from ***A Green Poetry Paintbox*** (Oxford University Press)

INFORMATION BOOKS

Building Site Carol Watson Busy Places series (Watts)
Find out about Glass, Find out about Plastic, Find out about Wool and Fibre Henry Pluckrose (Watts)
Bricks Terry Cash (A & C Black)
Wood Terry Jenkins (A & C Black)
Paper Annabelle Dixon (A & C Black)

STORY BOOKS

Window Jeannie Baker (Julie MacRae Books)
Harvey Hare: Postman Extraordinaire Bernadette Watts (North South Books)
The School Trip Nick Butterworth and Mick Inkpen (Hodder & Stoughton)
Mucky Pup Ken Brown (Andersen Press)
Something for James Shirley Isherwood and Neil Reed (Hutchinson)
The Do It Yourself House That Jack Built John Yeoman and Quentin Blake (Puffin Books)
This is our house Michael Rosen (Walker)
Through the Magic Mirror Anthony Browne (Hamish Hamilton)
Monkey Tricks Camilla Ashforth (Walker Books)
Alfie Gives A Hand Shirley Hughes (The Bodley Head)
The Toymaker Martin Waddle and Terry Milne (Walker)
Angel Mae Shirley Hughes (Walker)
Scared of a Bear Hilda Offen (Hodder Children's Books)

USEFUL ADDRESSES

Veritas, Lower Avenue, Leamington Spa, Warwickshire CV31 3NP. Tel: 01926 451730
St Paul's Multi Media, 199 Kensington High Street, London W8 6BA. Tel: 0171 937 9591